Shakara Bridgers,
Jeniece Isley, and
Joan A. Davis

Recipe Consultant
Therese Nelson

The
Get 'Em Girls'
Guide to the Power
of Cuisine

Perfect Recipes
for Spicing Up
Your Love Life

A Fireside Book
Published by Simon & Schuster

New York   London   Toronto   Sydney

Fireside
A Division of Simon & Schuster, Inc.
1230 Avenue of the Americas
New York, NY 10020

First Fireside trade paperback edition August 2008

FIRESIDE and colophon are registered trademarks of Simon & Schuster, Inc.

For information about special discounts for bulk purchases,
please contact Simon & Schuster Special Sales at 1-800-456-6798 or
business@simonandschuster.com.

Designed by Ruth Lee-Mui

Manufactured in the United States of America

2   4   6   8   10   9   7   5   3   1

Library of Congress Cataloging-in-Publication Data

Bridgers, Shakara.
The get 'em girls guide to the power of cuisine: perfect recipes for spicing up your love life /
Shakara Bridgers, Jeniece Isley, and Joan A. Davis.
p. cm.
"A Fireside Book."
1. Cookery, American—Southern Style.   2. Dating (Social customs)—United States.
I. Isley, Jeniece, 1977–   II. Davis, Joan A., 1981–   III. Title.
TX715.2.S68B73 2008
641.5975—DC22   2008022783

ISBN-13: 978-1-4165-8776-7
ISBN-10: 1-4165-8776-4

This book is dedicated to our mommies: *Deirdre, Jennifer,* and *Sandra.*

Acknowledgments

Jeniece

Thank you, Lord, for allowing me to see this dream come to fruition. God knows I fall short, and yet you still continue to bless me!

Mommy—The best cook in the *world*, for as long as I can remember, you have supported each and every one of my dreams; for that I thank you! I love you so much—you're the best! **Daddy**—I love you, and I know you are smiling on me. **Crystal**—You know you like my cooking, so stop fronting! Thank you for being the best sister a girl can ask for. **Kayla**—The world is a better place with you in it! You are the most talented and beautiful little girl I know; I couldn't have asked for a better niece. **Dee**—What can I say? You are my muse; thank you for letting me experiment on you. You will be my taste-tester forever—you are stuck with me! I love you, baby. **Shakara**—My business partner and best friend, you truly love hard girl, but I'm riding with you . . . all the way to *Oprah*! **Joan**—Thank you for being the balance, the voice of reason, the referee, and the confidante between Shakara and me. **Amithy**—Thank you for being the best friend a girl could ask for—and for blessing me with two beautiful godchildren. **Shanya** and **Justin**—I love you! **Nazae**—I'm a deadbeat godmommy, but I love you still! I'm going to get it right—I promise! **Danni**—We go through it, but I appreciate your friendship—you've put up with me for this long, I guess forever won't be so bad!

To the rest of my family: O-Mac—You are the most positive and hungry black man I've ever met . . . and I love you to death. **Rashein** and **Madisyn**—Love you! The entire **Isley Family**—Love you. **Dorian**—Continue to be the Lil' Diva that you are. **Bertina** and **Charlay**—Love you!

To my friends: **Pretty K**—From first grade to infinity! **Kirsten**, the make-up diva—Let's eat! **Badu**—Thank you for your encouragement . . . **Khalil**—Thanks for continuing to believe . . . now if only you'd get right, we could get you married! **Leah**—You are crazy as hell, but I can't imagine how I'd spend my days without you. **Dwayne**—"Much like the letter that Paul wrote to the Corinthians . . ." thank you for the love and *always* keeping it real! **PV**—Stay sweet. **Nancy**—Thank you for the advice and the beauty tips—is it prunes and moisturizer that keep you looking fabulous? **Russ** and **Cheryl**—Thank you for the support! **Guy**—You sent the first check in—so you know I got you! **Artie, Ernest,** and **Jose**—Thank you for always looking out for me!

To the ladies of **KLAD Creative, Kerry,** and **Leslie**—Thank you for jumping right in on this project and helping bring it to life—you two are the best! **Jennifer Cruté, illustrator extraordinaire**—Thank you for restoring our faith. You came right in and made it happen. **Terrell Belin**—You are a bad man—Thank you for all you do. **Wendy Catalano**—Thank you. **Therese Nelson**—You are the best at what you do. I wish you all the success in the world, and I want to be right there when you make your television debut! **Minah**—Thank you for always supporting me!

Joan

God, you did it once again for me; Father, I thank you for providing everything we needed to make this all possible. **My heartfelt thanks are extended to everyone** who supported me through this process with prayers and encouraging words; I thank you and send you my most sincere gratitude.

My love and thanks go out to my mom, who continuously believes in me, supports me, and challenges me to achieve greatness. Mommy, you are wonderful and I thank God for you daily. **To my late grandmother, Lilly Davis-Scott**—I know you are smiling down on me. **Aunt Tiny**—All your hard work has paid off; thanks for your love, patience, and recipes. **Aunt Jimetta and the boys**—Thanks for everything. **Aunt Swathavia**—You are the best and I love you! **The entire**

Davis family — You guys are so very special to me. It's because of you that I work as hard as I do. **Charles** and **Nicole Lynch** — Thank you for years of support and love.

Shakia Monique Knight — Thank you for seventeen years of friendship; your listening ear even from across the world means a lot to me. A very special thanks to **Pastor J. G. McCann** and **Mrs. McCann** who have instilled an immeasurable number of wisdom pearls into my life, and to the **St. Luke Nation** — Kin-Dom Achievers; may God shift you to greater heights as you move from vision to fruition. **Ms. Cookie** — You have supported us 100 percent and I'm truly grateful. **Jeniece** — Without a doubt, you are one of the most gifted women in this world; you can do anything you put your mind to do. **Shakara Bridgers** — Thank you for all that you've done for the success of this project. Your drive, determination, and competitive edge will keep you get anything you want out of life. **Yvette Fonéy** — You are a wonderful person and I thank God for blessing me with your friendship. **Shannon Tyson, Leslie Smalls, Deidrea McIntosh, Julia Baker, Steve Wright, Keith Reed, Margo Grant, Shalice Lloyd, Aureole Blanding, Vincent Johnson, Sharonda Williams, my "Gain and Loss Crew," my friends in the Operating Room** and at **East Side Tab** — You guys are simply the best and I love you! **Terrell Belin** of Belin Photography — This is only the beginning; the best is yet to come for you! **Kerry DeBruce, Jennifer Crute,** and **Wendy Catalano** — God sent you guys to us right in the nick of time.

Shakara

God — Thanks for your guidance; through you, all things are possible.

For so long I made up excuses as to why I didn't know how to cook; I feel so liberated now that I can!

Mommy — Thanks for always supporting me. You are my best friend. I am truly blessed to be your child. **Daddy** — I love you more than you know . . . more than I show. **Tanitsha** — I wouldn't trade you in for the world. You're my only sister; I love you. **Grandma** — You have always believed in me. You are so sweet and kind. It is my desire to be successful so that I can spoil you. **Great Grandma Beulah**—It's amazing how beautiful you still look at ninety! **Hilton**—Being a stepfather isn't always easy, but you make it seem effortless.

Aunt Renee, Aunt Andrea, Aunt Sharon, Aunt Joyce, Aunt Ann, Uncle Michael, Uncle Ricky, and **Uncle James**—Thanks for always looking out for me. Your guidance has helped me grow into a responsible woman. I love you all. **Andrenique** and **Cochise**—Hold tight. Your oldest cousin has got your back. **Damon**—I miss you. **Leonard**—Follow your dreams and you will always be successful. To the **Bridgers, Brown, Sherrod, Fonville,** and **Mills** families—I love you all, and thanks for being there for me throughout the years. **Jamal, CJ, Shannon, Steven, Cathy, Michelle, LaJohn, Mia, Ursula, Tory, Ryan,** and **Emika**—Thanks for being great cousins.

Moms—You are truly a rider. You have supported Jeniece, Joan, and me from day one. You have sacrificed so much for our success. Thanks for loving me as if I were your own.

Joan—Your passion for God moves me. You are a gentle person. Thanks for being my business partner and friend. **Jeniece**—What can I say? You are my friend for life. You are so talented; I have never seen you fail. I feed off your energy—it inspires me. I couldn't ask for a better business partner. **Satarah "Tori"**—You are my twin from another mother. It is not too often that you find someone you get along with all of the time. You are so strong and beautiful. I could not have made it through college without you. **Resonda**—Thanks for making me a godmother. I am so proud of you and Bunny. LB and Nakia Janee are so beautiful. **Tasha**—Girl, you are my heart. Just remember, I am here if you need me. **Crystal**—Slow down! I can never catch up with you.

LB, Nakia Janee, Morgan, Yalaina, Briana, Curtis, Corey, Javon, Davon, Rasheed, Rashad, Sydney, Sierra, and **Kayla**—You are the next generation. Enjoy being young! Listen to your parents and don't take any wooden nickels. I love all of you; call on me if you need me.

Peter "Guttaperk"—Thanks for always looking out for me. We have made money together and we have lost money together; throughout all of this we have remained friends.

Leah and Valerie—Thanks for being my friends. It is not too often that coworkers form true friendships. There will always be a job for you at Get 'Em Girl, Inc . . . lol!

Dee—People come and go, but you have always remained the constant. Your sacrifices are not in vain. Love ya, big brother!

Thanks to all of my friends who have supported me—**Jango, CL, Dwayne, Troy Marshall, Shawn "Tubby" Holiday, Gary, Cedric, Jeremy, Lavel, Beverly, Kyjuan, Ash, Amithy, Adri, Abdul, Benji, Damian (Brotha), Phoenix, Will, Deangelo, Delroy, Dirty, Dino, Donna, Koren, Kirsten, Tracy, Ellen, Jermaine, Tamir, Kim, Kandece, Don Baker, Lena, Lisa, Marcus and Natasha Kelly, Johnny "NuBuzz" Nunez, Mark, Vonnie, Veronica, JB, Spencer, Connell, Kasey "The Great," Autumn, Alice, Karima, Paul, Sasha, Oshea, JJ, Breon Olympia, Dr. Sean P. Gardner, Sr.,** and **The Eastward Baptist Church.**

Thanks to **Kerry, Leslie, Terrell, Wendy, Therese,** and **Jennifer** for seeing our vision and helping us create this beautiful book.

The Get 'Em Girls would like to thank

Trax Hair Salon (Tamika Goshay, you are the greatest hair stylist!), Cheryl, Tamir, Tasha Stoute, Brandi, Krista, Denada, Shyvonne, Nadeen, Noelle, Sheriser, Shani Kulture, Miss Jones and the Morning Show Crew, Mike Carter, Digiwaxx Media (CL and Neil, thanks for your support), Eric Nunlee, Tamika Nunley, True Control Fitness (Keisher and Lisa), NABFEME (Sheila and Johnnie), WEEN (Sabrina, Valeisha, Kristi), Nancy Taylor, Pooch, Sulay Hernandez and the Simon & Schuster staff, Elle, Miasha, DC Bookman (Tia), Chris Mercado, and **Minah.**

Contents

Oven-Fried Flounder
Sweet Potato Fries
"Spaghetti" with Meat Sauce
Yes-They're-Good-for-You Oatmeal Cookies

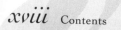

The Get 'Em Girls' Points to Remember

*i*f you're reading this, you have purchased this cookbook or are thinking about purchasing it. For that we thank you! When we decided to write this book we knew that we would get some strong supporters and some even stronger detractors. We just want to let you know that this book in no way, shape, or form, is meant to marginalize women. Our goal is to uplift women, to give them options. Dating is hard! We've tried everything else; why not try something that everyone can benefit from?

1. You Can't Get What Doesn't Want to Be Gotten!
Simply put, you can bake a peach cobbler that will bring tears to his eyes, but if he's not ready to be in a relationship, it is an exercise in futility. If you find that your efforts are constantly in vain and unappreciated, pick up your apron, dust the flour off your shoulders, and keep it moving.

2. You Have to Simmer Before You Boil!
Don't start with filet mignon and try to bring him back down to Steak-umm's—it won't work. Start slowly and pace yourself!

3. Don't Start What You Can't Finish!
Ladies, if you start out cooking seven days a week, he will expect you to cook seven days a week. Be as realistic as possible when making the decision to cook for

your potential love. This will save you the trouble of trying to break him out of daily dinners when, and if, he becomes your man.

Are you ready, ladies? Let's go get 'em!

Introduction

Get 'Em Girl: An ambitious woman who uses unconventional ways
to achieve her goals.

When we first decided to write this book, it was based solely on our love of three things: food, fun, and men! Being three single women living in New York City, we knew all too well, the pitfalls of dating in the big city. Young and career-oriented, we didn't have a real need (or desire) to cook. Yes, we had to eat, but this is New York! There is a restaurant, deli, or take-out place on every other block. However, we also knew that to date (and keep) a man in a place as big as New York, which is full of beautiful women of all backgrounds, we had to step up the game. We had to sit back and ask ourselves, "What are we bringing to the table?" Yes, we all are beautiful, intelligent, and educated—but so are the tens of thousands of other women waiting to take our places. So instead of trying to decipher what men want in a woman, we just asked them.

We set out with our list of questions and hit the streets (well, actually, the barbershops, supermarkets, churches, workplaces, and chat rooms) with one goal in mind: to find out what it is that men really want. While some definitely didn't want much (all you have to do is know how to drop it like it's hot and pick it up slow) almost all of them asked the inevitable, ". . . but can you cook?"

Now we have all heard the saying "The way to a man's heart is through his stomach," and most of us probably think it's an old-fashioned cliché that doesn't fit in this day and age. But as sure as the day is long, it's just as relevant today, if not more so, as it was fifty years ago. Contrary to how fine you know you are, any man is turned on by woman who is willing to invest the slightest bit of time and energy in pleasing him.

1

The purpose of this book is not to have women chained to the stove, but to reintroduce women to the art form of cooking, which, if done properly, can be easy, fun, and delicious. Just think about it: If you met a man at his place for a quiet evening, just to get to know each other, and found yourself presented with herb-roasted chicken, sautéed broccolini, and mushroom rice pilaf, you would be liable to lose all your religion and good sense — well, after you ate, of course. Aside from this being an immensely thoughtful thing to do, the fact that he dedicated the time to cook such an elaborate meal for you would probably send you right over the edge. Well — the same goes for him.

So with that said, if he's worth it, and if you're playing for keeps, impress him with that little thing you do with your tongue — and that little thing you do with your skillet.

10 Reasons to Cook for Your Man

1 You will have one more thing to impress him with. Of course he's turned on by your beautiful smile and sense of humor, but why not show him your other talents?

2 To add a little variety to an otherwise boring meal. Take him to the Caribbean on Tuesday and back to the Carolinas on Wednesday. Change is good—especially when it's good food!

3 Because you are a show-off! There is nothing wrong with tooting your own horn; hell, if you don't do it, no one will. Show him that you're out of the ordinary!

4 Cooking can be fun and flirtatious! Try wearing a very sexy outfit and heels while you serve him and watch how he responds to you.

5 You have to eat too! We know it sounds basic, but it's the truth. You can save a lot of money by cooking your own dinner and taking leftovers to work. No matter why you choose to cook, it's a win–win situation for you.

6 We're sure you can find better things to do with the money spent dining out every night. Eating out every now and then is cool; however, eating out daily can be expensive and mundane. Don't let your man get too accustomed to other people serving him.

7 How else can he give that star-studded performance that you are accustomed to? Just as a car can't run without fuel, neither can your man. If you expect mind-blowing performances, then make sure you give him the nourishment he needs to step up to the plate.

8 **He deserves it.** You realize you've got a keeper. Show him how much he is appreciated.

9 You love him way more than the delivery guy. Aside from quickly becoming boring and expensive, take-out is the easy way out and should always be the last resort.

10 Last but not least—you are a Get 'Em Girl! No explanation needed!

Plan of Action

*i*f the thought of cooking is frightening to you, we are here to tell you not to fret. Not everyone has the innate knowledge of how to cook—some of us chose to sit and watch our parents, while the rest of us picked up every book we could find on how to re-create our favorite dishes. No matter what method you choose to follow when getting your feet wet in the kitchen, there are some basics guidelines to stocking up and being prepared.

First and Foremost

Before you begin, make sure you read each recipe and menu thoroughly. This will help you to get acquainted with the ingredients, tools needed, and recipe steps.

Take Stock

Making sure that you always have the basic staples to whip up the perfect "in-no-time" meal is key. You will save yourself a world of headaches by always keeping a few key ingredients in stock. For instance, canned beans, tomato sauce, chili powder, and ground cumin can be whipped up in an instant—into a hearty vegetarian chili!

Take Shortcuts When Necessary

Although the premise of this book is about going back to basics, we are realists—and realistically, there are times when shortcuts just make better sense. For instance, storebought marinara sauce works in a pinch. Yes, making your own sauce is ideal, but sometimes time just doesn't permit. Also, precut veggies are perfect to have in the freezer, just in case. Use your best judgment when taking shortcuts and you will be fine.

Quality over Quantity

Remember, you are preparing an intimate dinner for your potential mate, not a smorgasbord. Keep it simple and easy. You will find that three well-thought-out and creative dishes are worth more than ten thrown-together meals any day. Don't overwhelm yourself by trying to make every dinner a Thanksgiving meal. Before you know it, you'll be worn out and back to drive-through windows. Pace yourself!

Making Substitutions

If you see a recipe that you just absolutely have to try, but you are watching your calories, carbohydrates, or fat intake, try substituting some of the ingredients with their reduced-fat alternatives. It's really up to your taste—just play with it. You may have to adjust the seasoning, and the consistency of some of the dishes, but let your taste buds be the judge.

When All Else Fails, Go with What You Know!

Rome wasn't built in a day, and your cooking skills won't be, either. If you are pressed for time or if you are trying to make a big impression, stick to the basics.

Taking Stock

*n*ow that you've made the decision to cook for the man you are so crazy about, the last thing you need is for him to be on his way with expectations of a fabulous meal when you realize you have no curry powder for your Curried Chicken and Rice. Here is a list of staples that should be on hand in your refrigerator and pantry. Whether you want to whip up a quick meal for yourself or a little something for your man, you can choose which ingredients best fit your style of cooking.

Asian seasonings: soy sauce, teriyaki sauce, oyster sauce, hoisin sauce
Baking needs: double-acting baking powder, baking soda, extracts (vanilla, almond, lemon, etc.), flour (all-purpose, cake, and self-rising)
Beans and legumes: any type of canned and dried varieties that you like
Broth and stocks: chicken, vegetable, and/or beef
Butter: salted, unsalted
Caribbean seasonings: jerk seasoning, curry powder, browning, coconut milk
Cheeses: Parmigiano-Reggiano (shredded, cubed, or wedge), Cheddar, any other varieties you like
Condiments: mayonnaise, prepared mustard (Dijon and yellow), salsa, ketchup, hot pepper sauce, honey
Eggs: farm-fresh large
Fruit: lemons, limes, oranges
Garlic: whole, and chopped in oil
Grains: cornmeal, rice (brown, basmati, long-grain white, etc.), oatmeal
Herbs (dried): oregano, thyme, rosemary, Italian seasoning blend

Herbs (fresh): basil, flat-leaf parsley, mint, thyme, rosemary

Milk: condensed, evaporated, whole, low- or no-fat

Nuts: walnuts, pecans, almonds

Oil: extra virgin olive oil, vegetable oil, peanut oil, nonstick cooking spray

Onions: red and yellow onions, shallots, scallions

Pasta: long (fettuccine, spaghetti, etc.), short (rotini, macaroni, penne, etc.)

Potatoes: Red Bliss, Russet, Yukon Gold

Seafood (canned): tuna, salmon

Spices: cinnamon, chili powder, bay leaves, nutmeg, salt (kosher, iodized), pepper (whole black pepper, white pepper, and cayenne), seasoning blends (seafood and/or steak seasoning), Get 'Em Girls' Essential Seasoning (page 29)

Sugars: brown (light and/or dark), granulated (white), confectioners'

Tomatoes (canned): whole, crushed, paste

Vinegars: balsamic, red wine, distilled white

Equipment Check

You fight your way through the hustle and bustle of midtown traffic to get to your favorite department store—on a Wednesday, no less. You make your way to the "Cellar" and immediately get the chills. You realize just then that you've stepped into kitchen utopia and have absolutely no idea what you're looking for. Step to the side, let the other shoppers off the escalator, and take three deep breaths—feel better? Okay, let's get started. Ideally, you want heavy-bottomed pots and pans made of stainless steel—preferably with copper bottoms (copper conducts heat better than stainless steel, although it does require frequent polishing). The handles should be riveted to the pan and oven-safe—and don't forget the lids.

Small saucepan: holds approximately two quarts and is good for melting butter, warming milk, and reheating sauces

Medium saucepan: holds about four quarts and is great for making pasta sauces, rice, and small portions of soup

Large stockpot: holds about eight quarts and is ideal for cooking pasta, soups, and stews

Small skillet: for making omelets and toasting nuts

Medium skillet: for stir-frying and sautéing; consider getting a cast-iron skillet as well, for frying and browning

Large skillet (optional): great for large dishes like paella

Roasting pan: a must-have for slow roasting

Grill pan: just the right tool for indoor picnics

More Pots and Pans: The following baking dishes, pots, and pans are also essentials:

Dutch Oven
13 x 9-inch baking dish
2½-quart casserole
11 x 7-inch baking dish
Omelet (nonstick) pan
Wok
8 x 8-inch baking dish

If you intend on baking, here are a few basic essentials needed.

Round cake pans, 8- or 9-inch, with straight sides: you'll need three of these for that Red Velvet Cake you plan on making to go with that red velvet teddy you plan on wearing
Cookie sheets: everybody loves cookies, and you can't make them in a skillet
Springform pan, 9- or 10-inch: ideal for making cheesecakes and tortes
Muffin tin, 12-cup: well, for muffins
Wire cooling racks: just what you need to allow your baked goods to cool evenly
9-inch fluted tube pan (same as 12-cup, but easier to identify)
10-inch tube pan
9-inch pie pan
Rolling pin
10-inch round cake pans (2)
Assorted mixing bowls: useful for prepping for your baking projects as well as mixing batters
Measuring cups and spoons: it's all about precision and exact measurements with baking, so make sure you have dry and liquid measuring cups and all the right tools

You made it through cookware and bakeware and your hands are almost full, but you can't leave without knives. When you set out to get a knife set, you will probably be surprised at the range of prices and quality. The old adage "you get what you pay for" has never been more true than when you are shopping for knives. Be sure to purchase knives with high-carbon stainless steel blades. The handles should be riveted to the blade and they should feel slightly heavy and evenly weighted in your hand.

Chef's knife, 8- or 10-inch: personally, we are 10-inch girls, but purchase whichever is comfortable for you. Ideal for cutting meat and vegetables

Paring knife: a 3-inch blade is great for peeling and cutting fruits and vegetables

Serrated knife: great for slicing crusty bread loaves

Steak knives (optional): if you plan on making steak, these will come in handy—we promise

Sharpening steel: sharpens and realigns your knives

You may want to grab a cart for the next section—appliances and gadgets, baby! There are so many kitchen gadgets and appliances to choose from; they do everything from spin salads to peel potatoes. For now, keep it basic and use your better judgment when choosing which products are essential and which are just plain ridiculous. Here are a few that we think are essential to everyday cooking.

Food processor: durable and useful for everything from mixing pastry dough to grating cheese. You will wonder how you made it this far without one

Blender: great for smoothies, daiquiris, margaritas, daiquiris, coladas, oh— and daiquiris

Electric mixer: choose a stand or hand mixer; whichever your budget permits

Cutting boards: plastic boards are easier to clean and take care of but wood boards are so damn sexy! Periodically rub them down with mineral oil (we're still talking about cutting boards, freshy!) to keep your wood boards from cracking

Colander: essential for draining pasta and washing vegetables

More Appliances and Gadgets: The following gadgets are also essential to every-day cooking:

Pepper mill	Offset spatula
Wine rack	Skimmer or large cooking spoon
Whisk	Mesh strainer
Slotted spatula	2-quart pitcher
Silicone spatula	Serving platter(s)
Ladle	Pastry blender
Pincer-type tongs	Biscuit cutter/cookie cutter
Vegetable peeler	Serving bowls
Wooden spoons	Pastry brush
Slotted spoon	Roll of parchment paper
Cheese grater	Pot holders
Thermometer	Cheesecloth
Kitchen-grade fire extinguisher	Nutmeg grater

Is He Worth It?

*t*he day is here. You finally worked up the nerve to ask the handsome man you keep bumping into at the cleaners out for drinks, and it was a success! After weeks of restaurant hopping and movie dates you decide you want to invite him over for a nice home-cooked meal. Before you run out and spend your entire check at Whole Foods, or purchase that candy red KitchenAid mixer, ask yourself—is he worth it?

We understand he's cute and his body is to die for, but would he appreciate you sweating out your fresh 'do shucking oysters for homemade Oyster Bisque? (Okay—so you won't be shucking the oysters; you can leave that to your fishmonger, but he doesn't know that.) If the answer is yes, then call your hairstylist for an appointment and get in that kitchen! If you're not too sure, just ask yourself the following questions:

Was There a Connection?

Can you see yourself being in a quiet place with this man for hours, and not running out of things to talk about? Or did you find yourself sending S.O.S. text messages to your girlfriends to come save you from this hell called a date?

Can He Hold a Conversation?

Did he keep your attention? Was he a good listener? Was he engaging or evasive?

Was He Respectful?

Did he come to your door and pick you up for the date or did he call you from his car and tell you to be outside in five minutes? Did he damn near break his neck when the cute waitress walked by?

Does He Have a Sense of Humor?

Were you laughing at his jokes to spare his feelings? For one minute, did you wish Sandman Sims was around to pull his behind out of the restaurant?

Did He Arrive with Drama?

Was the baggage he brought to the table Ziploc or garbage bag–sized? When talking about his ex, did his left eye twitch unconsciously?

Is He Insecure?

Did you have to hear about his days as a semipro baller over and over? Was he trying too hard to impress you with stories about his famous ex-girlfriend?

Table 101

*t*here comes a time in a woman's life when TV tables will not do. This is one of those times. You are trying to make a lasting impression on the man that just may be your future, so pack up the plastic cups, push the paper plates to the back of the cupboard, and break out the matching service for four that you got as a housewarming gift.

Setting the Table

If your dining table is a hand-me-down disaster, an occasional table moonlighting as a dinette set, or if you just want to protect the furniture that you worked hard for, you may want to start with a tablecloth. They are simple enough to purchase; just hit up Linens-N-Things or Target. They come in so many cool styles and colors, just make sure you get the right shape and length for your table—and don't forget to iron it! Next, pick up a set of cloth napkins. Ideally, they should match or coordinate with your tablecloth. But if your own personal style dictates striped tablecloth and paisley napkins—do you! Napkin rings are a classy touch to the table setting, though definitely not necessary. If you're taking him on a Trip for Two to the Caribbean, tie a piece of natural raffia around the napkins for a cute (and cheap) play on your dinner's theme.

Light It Up!

Head over to Yankee Candle and pick up some pillar or tea light candles to create a mood-enhancing centerpiece. But don't get too candle crazy—shimmying down the fire escape in your 4-inch Giuseppe Zanottis isn't sexy.

Dishes, Glasses, Silverware — Oh My!

Once again, they should all match. Simple white plates are perfectly fine, and get some Oneida in your life and pick up a set of matching flatware as well. A set of wineglasses might set you back about fifty-two cents at Ikea, so get a couple of sets. But if you want glasses that can withstand more than four cycles in the dishwasher, you may want to pay a little more. Either way, make sure they match.

The illustration shown is a table setting for a casual dinner. There are more than a few ways to set a table, from basic to "this is ridiculous." We don't have enough table space for "this is ridiculous," so here you go. (smile)

1. Wine, water, or pineapple juice—whichever you prefer, the glass goes over the dinner knife.
2. Dinner plate should be placed in the center.
3. Remember those cloth napkins we mentioned earlier? Well, this is where they go, whether neatly folded into a rectangle or with a napkin ring.
4. Salad, anyone? This is the fork for it.
5. Set the dinner fork directly to the left of the plate, please.
6. Knives should be placed to the right of the plate with the cutting edge facing the dinner plate.
7. The spoon goes to the far right—yes, right there.

Wasn't that easy? All right, now that we have the table in order, let's work on the wine selection. Come on, you can do it!

Table 101 **17**

Wine Basics

$\mathcal{S}$electing the right wine to complement your meal can be a harrowing experience for a beginner, but a little knowledge can minimize the intimidation factor. In fact, wine choice should be based on what you like, first and foremost. To help you select the wine that best complements the meal you are preparing, there are some basic principles to go by. Generally, white wines go well with delicately flavored foods, while red wines often pair better with heartier meals. Ultimately, the decision is yours to make and should always be based on your personal taste.

We put together a list of popular whites and reds to help in choosing the perfect wine for your evening:

White Wines

Chablis (Sha-BLEE)
How does it taste: Refreshing but not overwhelming.
Pairs well with: Seafood, poultry, and salads with nonacidic dressing.

Chardonnay (Shar-doe-NAY)
How does it taste: Generally, chardonnays can range in flavor from the light and crisp applelike flavor of those from France to Australian chardonnays that have aromas of tropical fruit and honey.
Pairs well with: Pasta, shrimp, poultry, and mild fish varieties for the lighter wines; and pork, salmon, and tuna for the heavier varieties.

Gewurztraminer (Geh-VERTZ-trah-mee-nur)
How does it taste: Floral with aromas of nutmeg and cloves.

Pairs well with: Spicy Asian dishes go very well with the crisp varieties, while the sweeter varieties are best served with cheese or dessert.

Pinot Grigio/Gris *(PEE-noe GREE-joe/Gree)*

How does it taste: Pinot Grigio has a subtle taste, while Pinot Gris has a fruitier flavor.
Pairs well with: Roasted chicken or pork, shellfish, and eggs—especially omelets.

Riesling *(REEZE-ling)*

How does it taste: Has a well-balanced and subtle flavor of honey and fruit, which varies from dry to very sweet, depending on the origin and time of harvest.
Pairs well with: Steamed fish and spicy foods. Late-harvest varieties are good as a dessert wine.

Sauvignon Blanc *(SO-veen-yawn blahn)*

How does it taste: Dry, tart flavor with notes of citrus, melon, and passion fruit.
Pairs well with: Grilled seafood, poultry, vegetables, and spicy foods.

Red Wines

Bordeaux *(Bore-DOH)*

How does it taste: Fruity and light- to medium-bodied, or rich, complex, and full-bodied.
Pairs well with: Roasted red meats and chicken as well as spicy pasta.

Cabernet Sauvignon *(Cab-air-NAY So-veen-YAWN)*

How does it taste: Oaky, with a hint of blackberry, plum, and black cherry.
Pairs well with: Roasted or grilled red meats, turkey, and chicken.

Chianti *(Ki-AHN-tee)*

How does it taste: Light and easy wine with the taste of berries and hints of spice.
Pairs well with: Pizza, pasta, roasted chicken or fish, and steak.

Pinot Noir *(PEE-noe nwahr)*

How does it taste: Fruity, with hints of cherry, plum, and pepper.
Pairs well with: Chicken, pork, lamb, and salmon.

Rioja *(Ree-OH-hah)*

How does it taste: Fruity flavor of berries and plums with a hint of vanilla and spice.
Pairs well with: Mildly spicy Latin and Asian dishes as well as roasted meat, chicken, salmon, and tuna.

Sangiovese *(Sahn-joe-VAY-zeh)*

How does it taste: Spicy with hints of cherries, raspberries, and anise.
Pairs well with: Pasta, fish, seafood, and roasted meats.

Shiraz/Syrah *(Shee-RAHZ/See-RAH)*

How does it taste: Ripe and fruity, with a subtle spiciness.
Pairs well with: Pizza, chili, and roasted salmon.

Zinfandel *(ZIN-fahn-dell)*

How does it taste: Bright and spicy with a hint of plums, raspberries, or blackberries.
Pairs well with: Prime rib, sausages, chicken wings, and stews.

Food Labels Made Easy

*t*he labels found on food in the grocery stores can be very confusing. Here we break down the facts so you can make better food choices when shopping and eating.

Nutrition Facts

Serving Size 1 cup (228g)
Serving Per Container 2

Amount Per Serving

Calories 250	Calories from Fat 110

	% Daily Value*
Total Fat 12g	**18%**
Saturated Fat 3g	**15%**
Trans Fat 3g	
Cholesterol 30mg	**10%**
Sodium 470mg	**20%**
Potassium 700mg	**20%**
Total Carbohydrate 31g	**10%**
Dietary Fiber 0g	**0%**
Sugars 5g	
Protein 5g	

Vitamin A	4%
Vitamin C	2%
Calcium	20%
Iron	4%

* Percent Daily Values are based on a 2,000 calorie diet. Your Daily Values may be higher or lower depending on your calorie needs.

	Calories:	2,000	2,500
Total Fat	Less than	65g	80g
Sat Fat	Less than	20g	25g
Cholesterol	Less than	300mg	300mg
Sodium	Less than	2,400mg	2,400mg
Total Carbohydrate		300g	375g
Dietary Fiber		25g	30g

1. **Serving size:** This is a key piece of information when you are watching your portions. If you eat more than the serving size, the nutritional value changes as well.

2. **Calories:** Educate yourself on how many calories you should be eating on a regular basis. This information will help you when trying to lose weight by adopting a reduced-calorie meal plan.

3. **Total fat:** If it sounds like trouble, it may or may not be! There are bad fats (fats that raise LDL cholesterol and promote heart disease) and good fats (fats that don't raise, and may even lower LDL cholesterol). Moderate intake of all types of fat is best, to maintain a well-balanced diet. **Saturated fat:** This is the main dietary cause of high blood cholesterol and should be limited to 7% of your total daily calorie intake.

Trans fat: Found mostly in fast foods, margarine, beef, white breads, shortenings, and storebought cookies. It is believed to raise cholesterol levels more than saturated fats. Look for foods labeled "trans fat free" when possible. **Polyunsaturated and monounsaturated fat:** Found in olive, canola, sesame, and corn oils, these fats may help lower your blood cholesterol level when used in place of saturated fats.

4. **Sodium:** The recommended dietary intake for sodium is 2,400 to 3,000 mg per day, but if you're watching your blood pressure, or are suffering from high blood pressure, we suggest consuming a little less.

5. **Total carbohydrate:** When reading labels, make sure you look at the total grams of carbohydrates, instead of just the grams of sugar. Carbohydrates comprise starches and dietary fiber, as well as sugar—so read carefully.

It's Not His Mama's . . .
But It Comes Close

Shakara's Menu
Simple Southern-Fried Chicken
Baked Macaroni and Cheese
Get 'Em Girls' Essential Seasoning
Luscious Candied Sweets
Fresh Green Beans with Red Potatoes
Sticky Monkey Bread
Southern Girl Sweet Tea

Jeniece's Menu
So-Serious Suffocated Pork Chops
Buttery Rice
Collard Greens with Smoked Turkey Wings
Sweet Potato Biscuits
Simple and Sinful Banana Pudding
Lip-Puckering Lemonade

Joan's Menu
Fried Catfish Fillets
Not-His-Mama's Potato Salad
Fried Cabbage and Bacon
Southern-Fried Okra
Simply Sweet Cornbread
Red Velvet Cake
Half-and-Half with Lemonade Ice Cubes

You know how great a cook you are. People have been telling you for years that you could put more than a few "soul food" restaurants out of business if they tasted your blackberry peach cobbler. So the thought of your man coming over for a nice down-home dinner is a welcome challenge. In fact, you've been reading cookbooks all day to get just the right recipes down pat for your dinner with your baby, and when he gets there you know—wait, let's say that again—you *know* he's going to lose his mind over the meal you have planned for him.

You have been burning in the kitchen all day. You've got the greens and smoked turkey wings on simmer, the chicken frying to a golden crisp, and the macaroni and cheese bubbling in the oven. When you bring your man his plate you wait until he takes the first bite, and you eagerly ask, "How does it taste?" After all your hard work, what is his answer? "It's not my mama's, but it's good!" Ladies, I know at this point you want to snatch your plate back from his hands and go off on him, but don't! Contrary to the way it sounds, this is a compliment, and one that should be regarded highly.

You see, even the slightest comparison of your cooking to his mother's is a good thing. Consider this: When you think of your mom's cooking, aside from the taste, you probably think about memories that are some of the most enjoyable times of your life. Well, the same goes for him.

So the next time you bring him his plate and he looks up at you and makes that comparison, know that what he is actually saying to you is, "Are you trying to make me fall in love with you?" Smile slyly, and whisper softly . . . Get 'Em Girl!

Simple Southern-Fried Chicken

*t*here is absolutely nothing like good fried chicken. You will love the crispy coating of this chicken. Serve with a cold glass of Southern Girl Sweet Tea (page 33). If it's a *really* good evening serve him the leftovers, if there are any, with homemade Buttermilk Waffles (page 67) the next morning.

1 Clean and rinse the chicken under cold water. Place in a container and add the lemon juice, let sit for 1 minute, and rinse well with cold water. Pat dry and season with 1½ teaspoons salt and 1 teaspoon ground black pepper. Cover and refrigerate for at least 1 hour.

2 Place the flour in a resealable plastic bag and season with salt and pepper.

3 Mix the eggs and the milk in a wide shallow bowl, and season with salt and pepper. Dip the chicken pieces into the egg mixture, and then place each piece in the bag. Shake until chicken is completely coated. Set aside while the oil is heating.

4 In a large skillet, preferably cast iron, heat the oil over high heat until very hot, but not smoking, about 350°F. Carefully add chicken pieces, making sure not to overcrowd the skillet.

5 Fry chicken, uncovered, turning occasionally with tongs until golden brown on all sides and cooked throughout, about 6 minutes for breasts and wings, and 8 to 10 minutes for thighs and legs.

6 Remove the chicken from the skillet with a slotted spoon and drain on a paper towel-lined platter. Season with salt and pepper and cover with aluminum foil to keep warm while you cook the next batch.

Makes 4 servings

1 chicken (2½ to 3 pounds), cut into 8 pieces

½ cup lemon juice (about 5 lemons)

Salt and ground black pepper

1½ cups all-purpose flour

3 eggs

½ cup milk

Vegetable oil, for deep-frying

Baked Macaroni and Cheese

10 tablespoons unsalted butter, plus extra for the pan

1 pound (about 4 cups) elbow macaroni, uncooked

1 cup shredded mild Cheddar cheese

1 cup shredded sharp Cheddar cheese

½ cup shredded Monterey Jack cheese

1 pint half-and-half

One 10.75-ounce can Cheddar cheese soup (recommended: Campbell's)

2 large eggs, lightly beaten

1 teaspoon Get 'Em Girls' Essential Seasoning (following page)

½ teaspoon ground black pepper

*W*hile boxed mac and cheese may work if the man in your life just turned six, a grown man needs a little more. Layered with Monterey Jack and sharp and mild Cheddar cheeses, this version is sure to bring back memories of Sunday dinners at his mama's.

1 Preheat the oven to 350°F. Lightly butter a deep 2½-quart casserole dish.

2 Bring a large pot of salted water to a boil over high heat. Stir in the macaroni and cook until the macaroni is just tender, about 7 minutes. Do not overcook. Drain well and return to the pot.

3 Melt 8 tablespoons of butter in a small saucepan. Stir into the macaroni. In a large bowl, mix the Cheddar and Jack cheeses.

4 Stir into the macaroni the half-and-half, 2 cups of the cheese mixture, the soup, and the eggs. Season with the Seasoning and black pepper. Transfer to the buttered casserole. Sprinkle with the remaining ½ cup of cheese and dot with the remaining 2 tablespoons of butter.

5 Bake until casserole begins to bubble around the edges, about 35 minutes.

Makes 6 servings

MAKE IT YOUR OWN

Experiment with different cheeses. Add a ½ cup of asiago cheese for added bite, or substitute a ½ cup of pepper Jack for the Monterey to add a little kick!

Fresh Green Beans with Red Potatoes

*f*reeze! Step away from the canned goods and head over to the produce aisle. Anyone can open up a can of watered-down veggies; why not impress your man by cooking fresh green beans?

1 Remove the ends from the green beans. Place the beans into a colander and rinse with cold water. Drain completely and set aside.

2 Heat the olive oil in a large Dutch oven, preferably cast iron, over medium heat. Add the turkey wing; cook and stir for about 8 minutes.

3 Toss the green beans into the pot, stirring them with a wooden spoon to coat well with oil. Stir in the broth, Seasoning, pepper, and garlic powder. Cover tightly.

4 Cook over medium-low heat for about 25 minutes, or until the beans are half done.

5 Meanwhile, cut the potatoes in half and place in a bowl of cold water. After the beans have cooked for 25 minutes, drain the potatoes and add them and onions to the beans. Add ¼ cup more broth, if needed.

6 Cover and continue to cook until the potatoes are tender, 20 to 25 minutes, periodically checking to make sure a small amount of liquid remains.

7 When the potatoes are tender, remove the lid. Stir in the butter and season with additional Seasoning and pepper, if necessary. Separate turkey from bones and discard bones. Continue to cook until the green beans are wilted, about 10 minutes.

Makes 2 to 4 servings

1½ pounds fresh green beans

3 tablespoons olive oil

One 1-pound smoked turkey wing, whole

1 cup vegetable broth or water, plus more if needed

1 teaspoon Get 'Em Girls' Essential Seasoning (page 29), plus more to taste

¼ teaspoon ground black pepper, plus more to taste

¼ teaspoon garlic powder

6 small unpeeled red-skin potatoes, washed and scrubbed

¼ cup slivered onion

2 tablespoons unsalted butter

SHORTCUT Save yourself some time! If your supermarket has presnapped green beans, buy them! The expense isn't that much more, and you can spend the 20 to 30 minutes gained setting the stage for an unforgettable evening.

Sticky Monkey Bread

½ cup granulated sugar

2 teaspoons ground cinnamon

8 tablespoons butter

½ cup packed light brown sugar

1½ cups chopped pecans

Two 10-count cans refrigerated biscuits

*i*f you don't have time to bake an apple pie or a chocolate cake, try this quick fix that will have him hanging from the ceiling and begging for more!

1 Preheat oven to 350°F. Spray a 9-inch fluted tube pan with nonstick cooking spray.

2 Mix the granulated sugar and cinnamon together in a bowl and set aside.

3 In a small saucepan over low heat, melt the butter and brown sugar, stirring well. Remove from heat. Sprinkle ½ cup of the pecans into the bottom of the tube pan.

4 Toss the biscuits into the cinnamon-sugar mixture and set aside.

5 Layer half of the biscuits in the prepared tube pan, spoon half of the brown sugar mixture over the biscuits, and sprinkle with ½ cup of the pecans.

6 Repeat with the remaining biscuits, brown sugar mixture, and pecans.

7 Bake for about 25 minutes. Let stand for 5 minutes. Place a plate on top and invert. Serve warm.

Makes 8 servings

Southern Girl Sweet Tea

*W*hat better way to finish off a fabulous meal than with freshly brewed sweet tea!

1 Place the tea bags and baking soda in a 1-quart measuring cup. Pour the boiling water over the tea bags. Cover and steep for 15 minutes.

2 Remove the tea bags; do not squeeze. Pour the tea into a 2-quart pitcher.

3 Stir in the sugar until completely dissolved. Add cold water. Refrigerate until chilled. Serve over ice, garnished with mint leaves and lemon wedges.

Makes about 2 quarts

6 orange pekoe tea bags (recommended: Lipton or Luzianne)

⅛ teaspoon baking soda

2 cups boiling water

1½ cups sugar

6 cups cold water

Mint leaves, for garnish

Lemon wedges, for garnish

So-Serious Suffocated Pork Chops

½ cup vegetable oil

4 center-cut, bone-in pork chops, about 8-ounces each

Get 'Em Girls' Essential Seasoning (page 29)

Freshly ground black pepper

½ cup plus 2 tablespoons all-purpose flour

1 medium onion, chopped

1 cup cold water

¼ teaspoon garlic powder

*C*aution! If you are not interested in having him show up at your house unannounced, with empty plate in hand, then these pork chops are *not* to be played with! Serve them with Buttery Rice (following page) or Pure Bliss Mashed Potatoes (page 122) and the two of you might as well find a warm blanket and a comfy spot on the couch—because he won't be going anywhere! Try this recipe with turkey cutlets for an equally delicious version.

1 In a large heavy-bottomed skillet, heat the vegetable oil over medium-high heat. Season both sides of the pork chops with 1 teaspoon Seasoning and ½ teaspoon ground black pepper.

2 Place ½ cup flour in a bowl and season to taste with Seasoning and pepper. Coat the pork chops in flour, shaking off excess.

3 Using tongs, carefully place pork chops in the skillet. Cook until both sides are a golden brown, about 3 minutes per side. Transfer to a plate and cover loosely with aluminum foil to keep warm.

4 Pour off all but 1 tablespoon of oil, making sure not to pour off any of the flour bits at the bottom of the skillet. Reduce heat to medium and add the onion. Cook, stirring often, until softened, about 3 minutes. Sprinkle with the remaining 2 tablespoons of flour and stir well.

5 Cook until flour begins to brown. Stir in the water and bring to a simmer. Season to taste with Seasoning, pepper, and garlic powder.

6 Return the pork chops to the skillet. Reduce heat to medium-low and cover.

7 Cook, stirring occasionally, until the pork chops show no signs of pink when pierced at the bone, about 30 minutes.

Makes 4 servings

Buttery Rice

a Carolina staple—no Southern meal is complete without it.

1 In a medium saucepan, bring the water to a rapid boil over high heat. Add the rice, butter, salt, and pepper. Reduce the heat to low and cover tightly.

2 Simmer until the liquid is absorbed and the rice is tender, 20 to 25 minutes. Remove from heat and let stand, covered, for 5 minutes. Fluff the rice with a fork and serve hot.

Makes 6 to 8 servings

1 quart water

2 cups uncooked long-grain white rice

4 tablespoons unsalted butter

1 teaspoon salt

½ teaspoon ground white pepper

Collard Greens with Smoked Turkey Wings

2 smoked turkey wings, cut up

1 tablespoon Get 'Em Girls' Essential Seasoning (page 29)

1½ teaspoons ground black pepper

1 teaspoon hot pepper sauce (optional)

3 bunches collard greens

1½ teaspoons sugar

⅛ teaspoon baking soda

*N*o Southern meal is complete without a tall glass of Lip-Puckering Lemonade (page 39) and a side of good ole' collards. These mean greens will definitely bring him back for seconds, thirds, and fourths!

1 Bring 3 quarts of water to a boil in a large pot over medium-high heat. Stir in the smoked turkey wings, Seasoning, black pepper, and hot pepper sauce (if using). Reduce the heat to medium; cover and cook until tender, about 1 hour.

2 In the meantime, wash the collard greens thoroughly in a sink full of cold water. Lift the greens out of the sink and transfer to a large bowl, allowing the grit to fall to the bottom of the sink. Repeat as necessary, until no grit remains.

3 Remove the thick stem that runs down the center of the greens by holding a leaf in one hand and stripping the leaf down with the other. Stack 6 to 8 stripped leaves on top of each other, roll up, and slice into ½- to 1-inch-thick slices.

4 Add the collard greens, sugar, and baking soda to the pot. Reduce the heat to low, partially cover, and cook, stirring occasionally, just until greens are tender, 30 to 45 minutes. Remove turkey meat and discard bones. Serve immediately with additional hot pepper sauce, if desired.

Makes 4 servings

Sweet Potato Biscuits

*W*ho knew sweet potatoes were good for more than pies?

1 Preheat oven to 400°F.

2 Bring a large pot of water to a boil. Thoroughly wash and scrub the sweet potatoes and peel. Cut sweet potatoes into 1½-inch chunks and add to the boiling water. Simmer for 20 minutes or until fork tender. Drain well and transfer to a large bowl. Mash with a potato masher and set aside to cool.

3 Beat the sugar, egg, and melted butter into the cooled, mashed sweet potatoes until smooth. Stir in milk and set aside.

4 In a separate bowl, sift together the flour and baking powder. Cut in shortening with a fork or pastry blender until mixture resembles small peas.

5 Make a well in the center of the dry mixture. Stir in the sweet potato mixture with a fork to make a soft dough.

6 Place the dough on a lightly floured work surface and knead gently, just until the surface of the dough isn't sticky, about 10 strokes.

7 Roll or pat dough into a ½-inch-thick disk. Cut with a floured 2½-inch biscuit cutter. Reroll as necessary. Place biscuits 1 inch apart on an ungreased cookie sheet.

8 Bake for 15 to 20 minutes, until the biscuits are lightly browned. Serve hot with butter.

Makes 16 biscuits

2 medium orange-flesh sweet potatoes

¼ cup sugar

1 large egg, beaten

1 tablespoon unsalted butter, melted

1 cup milk

3 cups self-rising flour, plus extra for kneading

1 teaspoon baking powder

½ cup vegetable shortening

Butter, for serving

TAKE NOTE

If you begin cooking and realize you do not have any self-rising flour, simply add 1½ teaspoons baking powder and ½ teaspoon salt to each cup of all-purpose flour.

Simple and Sinful Banana Pudding

One 3.4-ounce package instant vanilla pudding mix

2 cups cold milk

One 14-ounce can sweetened condensed milk

1½ teaspoons vanilla extract

One 8-ounce container frozen whipped topping, thawed

One 16-ounce package vanilla wafer cookies

12 ripe bananas, peeled and sliced

a classic dessert made super easy. Instant pudding teamed with sweetened condensed milk makes a perfect combination that saves you all the trouble of making homemade custard.

1 In a large bowl, beat the pudding mix and milk with an electric mixer on low until the mixture begins to thicken, about 2 minutes. Beat in the condensed milk and vanilla extract until smooth.

2 With a silicone spatula, gently fold in the whipped topping.

3 Spread a small amount of the pudding mixture on the bottom of a trifle dish or glass bowl and cover with a layer of cookies. Top with a layer of sliced bananas. Spoon ⅓ of the custard over bananas.

4 Continue layering cookies, bananas, and custard to make three layers of each, ending with custard. Cover with plastic wrap and chill until ready to serve.

Makes 8 servings

Lip-Puckering Lemonade

*t*his delicious lemonade reminds us of summers in the Carolinas with our grandparents! Enjoy!

1 In a 2-quart pitcher, combine the lemon juice and sugar, stirring continuously to dissolve the sugar.

2 Add the cold water and blend well.

3 Serve over ice. Garnish with lemon wedges.

Makes about 2 quarts

Juice of 8 large lemons, about 1 cup

1 cup sugar, or to taste

7 cups cold water

Ice cubes

Lemon wedges, for garnish

Fried Catfish Fillets

Vegetable oil, for frying

4 catfish fillets, about 4 ounces each, skin removed

Get 'Em Girls' Essential Seasoning (page 29)

Ground black pepper

⅔ cup milk

1 large egg

1 cup yellow cornmeal

½ cup all-purpose flour

Dash of cayenne pepper

Salt

Lemon wedges, for serving

Hot pepper sauce, for serving

*t*he key to good catfish is making sure the fish is as fresh as possible and the oil is the right temperature. This crunchy and light dish can be eaten as an appetizer or entrée.

1 Pour about 3 inches of oil into a large heavy skillet, preferably cast iron, and heat to 375°F.

2 Season both sides of the catfish fillets with 1 teaspoon Seasoning and 1 teaspoon black pepper. Mix the milk and egg together in a wide shallow bowl, and season to taste with Seasoning and black pepper. In a separate bowl, mix the cornmeal, flour, and cayenne. Season with additional Seasoning and black pepper to your taste.

3 One piece at a time, dip the catfish in the milk mixture and then coat in the cornmeal mixture, making sure to cover the fillets completely. Carefully add the fish to the hot oil in batches so the pan is not overcrowded.

4 Fry the fish for 3 to 5 minutes and then remove and drain on a paper towel–lined platter. Season immediately with a pinch of salt and black pepper. Serve hot with lemon wedges and hot pepper sauce.

Makes 2 to 4 servings

Not-His-Mama's Potato Salad

*l*ike a hug from your man after a long day, there is something comforting about potato salad. Okay, it's not that serious — but this potato salad is *good*!

1 Bring a large pot of water to a boil over high heat. Add the potatoes. Cook until tender, about 25 minutes. Drain and rinse under cold running water until cool enough to handle. Peel the potatoes and cut into medium cubes.

2 Combine the potatoes, onions, pickle relish, and eggs in a large bowl.

3 Season the potato mixture with Seasoning, black pepper, onion powder, garlic powder, and sugar. In a separate bowl mix together the mayonnaise, mustard, and vinegar. With a silicone spatula or wooden spoon, gently fold the mayonnaise mixture into the potato mixture, making sure not to break up the potatoes. Cover and chill in the refrigerator for several hours before serving.

Makes 4 to 6 servings

TAKE NOTE

For hard-cooked eggs, place the eggs in a pot of cold water and bring to a full boil. Cover tightly and remove from heat. Let stand for 10 full minutes in the hot water; this will help to prevent that ugly yellow line that forms when eggs are overboiled. After 10 minutes, drain and allow to cool. Once cool enough to handle, peel and use as directed.

4 to 6 large unpeeled Russet potatoes, washed and scrubbed

1 small yellow onion, finely chopped

½ cup sweet pickle relish, drained

4 hard-cooked eggs (see note), peeled and chopped

2 teaspoons Get 'Em Girls' Essential Seasoning (page 29)

1½ teaspoons ground black pepper

½ teaspoon onion powder

¼ teaspoon garlic powder

1 teaspoon sugar

1½ cups mayonnaise

2 tablespoons prepared yellow mustard

1 teaspoon distilled white vinegar

Fried Cabbage and Bacon

3 slices bacon

1 tablespoon unsalted butter

One (2½- to 3-pound) green head of cabbage, washed and coarsely chopped

¼ teaspoon Get 'Em Girls' Essential Seasoning (page 29)

¼ teaspoon ground black pepper

½ teaspoon sugar

¼ cup water

¼ teaspoon distilled white vinegar (optional)

1 Cook the bacon in a large pot over medium heat, until crisp. Remove the bacon from the pot. Drain, crumble, and set aside.

2 Add the butter to the pot. Carefully add the cabbage, stirring well to coat the leaves in the bacon and butter mixture. Add the Seasoning, black pepper, sugar, water, and vinegar (if using) to the pot and cover with a tight-fitting lid. Cook over medium heat for 10 to 15 minutes.

3 Remove the lid and scatter the crumbled bacon over the top of the cabbage. Cover and cook for an additional 3 to 5 minutes. Serve hot.

Makes 4 to 6 servings

Southern-Fried Okra

*a*lso known as "Southern popcorn." Fry up a batch and pop in his favorite movie. Make it a movie night he won't soon forget.

1 Mix the cornmeal and flour together in a medium bowl. Season to taste with salt and pepper.

2 In a separate bowl, combine the okra and buttermilk. Let marinate for 15 minutes.

3 Meanwhile, pour the vegetable oil into a large heavy skillet, preferably cast iron, and heat to 350°F.

4 Drain the okra and toss with the cornmeal mixture to coat well.

5 In batches, carefully add the okra to the hot oil and cook until golden brown.

6 Remove from the oil with a slotted spoon and drain on a paper towel–lined platter. Season with salt and pepper while hot and serve immediately.

Makes 6 to 8 servings

½ cup cornmeal

½ cup all-purpose flour

Salt and ground black pepper

2½ pounds fresh okra, sliced ½ inch thick (5 cups)

1 cup buttermilk

2 cups vegetable oil

Simply Sweet Cornbread

1 cup all-purpose flour

1 cup yellow cornmeal

⅔ cup sugar

1 teaspoon salt

1 tablespoon baking powder

2 large eggs

1 cup milk

⅓ cup vegetable oil

3 tablespoons unsalted butter, melted

Butter, for serving

Honey, for serving (optional)

*S*weet, crumbly cornbread that is so good it will melt in your mouth.

1 Preheat the oven to 400°F. Spray or lightly grease a 9-inch cast-iron skillet or cake pan.

2 Combine flour, cornmeal, sugar, salt, and baking powder in a large bowl.

3 In a separate bowl, lightly beat the eggs. Stir in the milk, vegetable oil, and butter until well mixed. Slowly stir the egg mixture into the corn-meal mixture and mix just until combined. Pour the batter into pre-pared skillet.

4 Bake for 20 to 25 minutes, until a toothpick inserted into the center of the cornbread comes out clean. Serve with additional butter and honey (if using).

Makes 12 servings

Red Velvet Cake

*S*lip on that red dress Johnny Gill sang about and serve him up a slice of cake. My, my, my!

1 Preheat oven to 350°F. Butter and flour three 8-inch round cake pans and set aside.

2 Cream the butter and sugar together in a large mixing bowl, using an electric mixer on high speed. Beat until light and fluffy, about 3 minutes. Add the eggs one at a time, and mix well after each addition.

3 In a small bowl, mix the cocoa and food color. Add to the sugar mixture and mix well.

4 Sift the flour and salt together into another large bowl. Slowly add the flour mixture to the sugar mixture alternately with the buttermilk. Beat in the vanilla. Combine baking soda and vinegar in a small bowl and add to mixture. Pour the batter into the prepared pans.

5 Bake until the top springs back when pressed lightly in the center, 20 to 25 minutes. Remove from heat and cool completely on a wire rack before frosting.

6 For the frosting: Using an electric mixer on high speed, blend the cream cheese and butter together in a large mixing bowl until smooth. Lower the mixer speed to low and add the marshmallow creme, extracts, and confectioners' sugar, and blend just until combined.

7 Unmold the cake layers. Spread the frosting evenly between layers and on top and sides of cooled cake. Garnish with crushed pecans around the sides of the cake, if desired.

Makes 16 to 20 servings

Cake

2 sticks (½ pound) unsalted butter, room temperature, plus extra for the pan

2 cups sugar

2 large eggs, room temperature

1 tablespoon Dutch-processed cocoa powder

2 tablespoons red food color

2½ cups cake flour

1 teaspoon salt

1 cup buttermilk, room temperature

1 teaspoon vanilla extract

½ teaspoon baking soda

1 tablespoon distilled white vinegar

Frosting

One 8-ounce package cream cheese, room temperature

8 tablespoons unsalted butter, room temperature

1 cup marshmallow creme (recommended: Fluff)

¼ teaspoon vanilla extract

¼ teaspoon almond extract

One 1-pound box confectioners' sugar

1 cup crushed pecans (optional)

Half-and-Half with Lemonade Ice Cubes

5 cups Lip-Puckering Lemonade
(page 39)

4 cups Southern Girl Sweet Tea
(page 33)

Lemon wedges, for garnish

*t*his is the best of both worlds, sweet, sour, and delicious!

1 Fill an ice cube tray with 1 cup of the lemonade and freeze until solid.

2 Transfer the lemonade ices cubes to a large pitcher. Pour the tea and the remaining lemonade over the ice cubes and stir to blend. Serve, garnished with lemon wedges.

Makes about 2 quarts

Grown 'n' Sexy

So Seductive Menu
Pairs Well With: Chardonnay

Oyster Bisque

Salmon with Brown Sugar Glaze

Sautéed Garlic Asparagus

Kiss o' Honey Potatoes

Hazelnut Chocolate–Dipped Strawberries

Simple 'n' Sexy Menu
Pairs Well With: Cabernet Sauvignon

Balsamic-Glazed Roast Chicken

Easy Like . . . Slow-Roasted Beef and Potatoes with Gravy

Broccoli with Garlic and Parmesan

Savory Rice

Easy Strawberry Shortcake

Sensual Substitutes

Fettuccine Alfredo with Shrimp

Herb-Crusted Sirloin

Roasted Garlic Fingerling Potatoes

Homemade Vanilla Ice Cream with Brown Sugar Peaches

> If the meal is good I'm always appreciative, if the meal is bad . . . it's the thought that counts. Just knowing that she wants to please me is what matters.
> —Jerry Green *New York, NY*

*a*fter five dates, two dozen roses, and six walks in the park, you've decided to invite him over for a nice dinner at your place. You've got the wine on ice, candles lit, Floetry playing, and the Victoria's Secret nightie tucked away in your bottom drawer waiting for the right moment to make its appearance—this is not a take-out night!

Call all of your girls and let them know you are not to be disturbed. Run through your checklist to make sure you have everything needed to make this a memorable, delicious, and safe evening.

Now that you have covered all of the basics, it's time to prepare the meal. You try to remember all of the foods that he mentioned he likes, whether he's allergic to seafood or if it's his favorite dish; if he is a meat and potatoes guy or a vegetarian—and you plan accordingly.

The recipes included in this section consist of foods that are not only delicious, but are known for their amorous effect on the body, which will make it an evening both of you will never forget.

The Get 'Em Girls' Grown 'n' Sexy Checklist

☐ ## Safety First!

Ladies, we know this is a cookbook, and condoms and Cornish hens don't mix—but we're saying it anyway!

☐ ## Good Sheets!

What makes a quality sheet, you ask? Hmm, let's see—the material, preferably 100 percent cotton; the thread count, ideally, two hundred and up; and the hand, basically how it feels against your skin. If you are a tee shirt-and-panties kind of girl or if your budget is tight, a good set of jersey sheets will do just fine! Oh, and have an extra pillow, just in case you don't want to share the four you have on your bed!

☐ ## Candles!

Pillar, tea light, soy, or gel . . . the choices and fragrances are endless.

☐ ## An Extra Toothbrush!

Morning breath is not cute, so be considerate and hook him up!

Oyster Bisque

Three 8-ounce containers shucked oysters in their own liqueor

Kosher salt

Ground white pepper

¼ cup finely chopped celery

3 tablespoons minced shallots (2 shallots)

¼ cup water

1 quart half-and-half

3 tablespoons unsalted butter

1½ teaspoons all-purpose flour

Hot pepper sauce

Chopped fresh flat-leaf parsley, for garnish

a hearty and thick soup. Serve in a crusty bread bowl, and turn this simple soup into an elegant start to a great dinner.

1 In a medium pot over low heat, combine the oysters and the oyster liqeuor with a pinch of salt and white pepper, and cover. Cook and stir occasionally until the edges of oysters begin to curl, about 5 minutes.

2 Remove the oysters from the pot with a slotted spoon and set aside. Add the celery, shallots, and water. Cook and stir until tender. Transfer the celery mixture, with the liquid, to a medium bowl and stir in the half-and-half. Set aside.

3 Melt the butter over low heat and whisk in the flour to make a roux. Add the celery mixture to the roux and stir until it begins to thicken.

4 Place oysters on a cutting board and chop into bite-size pieces; stir into the thickened oyster stock and season to taste with hot pepper sauce. Serve immediately, garnished with chopped parsley.

Makes 4 servings

APHRODISIAC ALERT!

Oysters! Ask Casanova—this is the ultimate passion food!

Salmon with Brown Sugar Glaze

*t*his seductive and sexy salmon dish is glazed with brown sugar and a hint of Dijon mustard. This is the ultimate date dish to prepare whenever you finally decide to cook for your beau. I make this dish and watch men instantly fall in love with me time after time. —*Joan*

1 In a small saucepan over medium-high heat, melt the brown sugar, honey, and butter. Remove from heat and whisk in the mustard, soy sauce, olive oil, and ginger. Set aside.

2 Preheat a grill pan over medium heat. Brush the salmon with vegetable oil and season to taste with salt and pepper.

3 Place the salmon skin side down in the grill pan. Brush the flesh of the salmon fillets with the brown sugar mixture. Grill for 6 to 8 minutes for medium doneness, turning once after 5 to 6 minutes. Remove from pan and serve immediately, flesh side up.

Makes 2 to 4 servings

APHRODISIAC ALERT!

Ginger! Egyptians used it to ward off impotence—you can use it to kick up your salmon (smile).

2 tablespoons light brown sugar

2 teaspoons honey

2 tablespoons unsalted butter

3 tablespoons Dijon mustard

4½ teaspoons soy sauce

4½ teaspoons olive oil

2 teaspoons minced dry ground ginger

4 salmon fillets, about 6 ounces each

Vegetable oil

Salt and ground black pepper

Sautéed Garlic Asparagus

3 tablespoons unsalted butter

2 cloves garlic, chopped

1 bunch (about ½ pound) fresh asparagus, tough ends removed

¼ teaspoon kosher salt

¼ teaspoon ground black pepper

*t*wo powerful passion foods combined makes for an explosive and delicious meal. Tread lightly.

1 Melt the butter in a large skillet over medium-high heat. Once the butter is melted, add the garlic, asparagus spears, salt, and pepper.

2 Cover and cook, stirring occasionally, until the asparagus is tender, about 10 minutes.

Makes 4 servings

APHRODISIAC ALERT!

Asparagus! Most erotic member of the vegetable family—particularly stimulating for men!

Garlic! Promotes virility, strength, and bad breath—make sure you have mints on hand!

Kiss o' Honey Potatoes

*t*he slight sweetness of these potatoes will complement any meal you prepare.

1 Preheat oven to 375°F. Lightly coat an 11 x 7-inch baking dish with nonstick cooking spray.

2 Arrange potatoes in a single layer in the prepared dish, top with the onion, and season with salt and pepper.

3 In a small bowl, combine melted butter, honey, and dry mustard. Drizzle over the potatoes and onion; stir to coat the potatoes.

4 Bake until tender and golden brown, 40 to 45 minutes, stirring halfway through the cooking time. Serve immediately.

Makes 4 servings

1 pound small unpeeled red potatoes, scrubbed and halved

2 tablespoons finely chopped sweet onion

¼ teaspoon salt

¼ teaspoon ground black pepper

3 tablespoons unsalted butter, melted

2 tablespoons honey

1 teaspoon dry mustard

APHRODISIAC ALERT!

Honey! Sweet, sticky, and perfect for drizzling—so addictive, it should come with an age limit!

Hazelnut Chocolate–
Dipped Strawberries

1 cup hazelnut chocolate spread
(recommended: Nutella)

1 tablespoon heavy cream

1 pint fresh strawberries, stems
intact, washed, patted dry, and
thoroughly air-dried

*W*ho doesn't love the taste of chocolate and strawberries? Well, we took this delicious dessert a step further by covering ripe, sweet strawberries in rich hazelnut chocolate spread. For an intoxicatingly sweet twist, inject the strawberries with a shot of hazelnut liqueur, such as Frangelico!

1 In a small bowl, vigorously whisk together the hazelnut chocolate spread and the cream until it reaches the consistency of melted chocolate. Set aside.

2 Carefully spear strawberries with toothpicks. Working quickly, swirl each strawberry gently in the chocolate mixture, about halfway up the fruit. Place the strawberries on a parchment paper–lined platter. Serve immediately or chill in the refrigerator to harden slightly.

Makes 4 servings

APHRODISIAC
ALERT!

Chocolate! Said to release the same chemical that the brain releases during sex! So that's why it's so good!

Strawberries! Don't they just look sexy? You feel sexier when eating them—we know!

Balsamic-Glazed Roast Chicken

Chicken seasoned with aromatic fresh rosemary and drizzled with a sweet balsamic glaze adds a wonderful twist on basic roasted chicken. Serve with Savory Rice (page 58).

1 Preheat the oven to 375°F.

2 Remove the giblets from the chicken and discard. Rinse the chicken well, inside and out, under cold water. Pat the chicken dry with paper towels, being sure to dry the body cavity as well.

3 In a small bowl, mix together the rosemary, garlic, poultry seasoning, salt, and pepper. Place the chicken on a rack in a roasting pan just large enough to hold the chicken.

4 Season the inside of the chicken with half of the herb mixture. Rub the melted butter and olive oil over chicken. Season the outside of the chicken with the remaining herb mixture.

5 Roast uncovered, basting with the pan juices every 15 minutes, until a meat thermometer inserted in the thickest part of the thigh reads 170°F, about 1½ hours.

6 Meanwhile, mix together in a small bowl the balsamic vinegar and the light brown sugar. Set aside.

7 Transfer the chicken to a serving platter. Drizzle with the balsamic vinegar mixture. Carve and scatter with rosemary sprigs.

Makes 4 servings

1 roasting chicken, 4½ pounds

1 tablespoon chopped fresh rosemary, about 2 sprigs, plus extra sprigs for garnish

1 clove garlic, chopped

1 teaspoon poultry seasoning

½ teaspoon kosher salt

1 teaspoon ground black pepper

3 tablespoons unsalted butter, melted

1 tablespoon olive oil

3 tablespoons balsamic vinegar

½ teaspoon light brown sugar

Easy Like . . . Slow-Roasted Beef and Potatoes with Gravy

One (3½-pound) bottom round or rump roast

1 teaspoon Get 'Em Girls' Essential Seasoning (page 29), plus more to taste

½ teaspoon ground black pepper, plus more to taste

¼ teaspoon garlic powder

3 tablespoons vegetable oil

1 medium onion, thinly sliced

3 sprigs fresh thyme

3 cups low-sodium beef broth

8 small unpeeled red-skin potatoes, scrubbed

2 tablespoons cornstarch

¼ cup water

Succulent oven-roasted beef with a delicious gravy seasoned with thyme, onions, and garlic. A great recipe for a Sunday dinner date with the man of your dreams.

1 Preheat oven to 275°F.

2 Season the beef on all sides with the Seasoning, black pepper, and garlic powder. In a large Dutch oven, heat the vegetable oil over medium-high heat. Add the beef and brown on all sides, about 4 minutes per side. Transfer the meat to a plate and set aside.

3 Stir in the onion slices and thyme sprigs and cook until the onions are tender, about 3 minutes. Return the meat to the pot, fat side up. Add the beef broth and place in the oven, uncovered.

4 Roast for 1 hour and remove from the oven. Add the potatoes to the pot; cover and return to the oven. Continue roasting until the beef is tender and the internal temperature registers 130° to 135°F, 30 to 40 minutes.

5 Remove from the oven. Using a slotted spoon, transfer the roast to a cutting board and the potatoes to a serving platter and let rest for 15 minutes before carving. Discard the onions and thyme sprigs.

6 While the roast is resting, in a small bowl, mix the cornstarch and water until dissolved. Place the Dutch oven over medium-high heat and gradually stir the cornstarch mixture into the remaining liquid. Bring to a boil.

7 Reduce the heat and continue to cook, stirring constantly until thickened, about 3 minutes. Season to taste with Seasoning and black pepper. Remove from heat and transfer to a gravy boat or decorative bowl.

8 Carve the roast and arrange the slices on a large platter. Arrange the potatoes around the roast and drizzle gravy over each portion. Serve immediately. Refrigerate leftovers for up to 5 days.

Makes 6 to 8 servings

Broccoli with Garlic and Parmesan

1 In a large skillet over medium-high heat, bring ¼ cup of lightly salted water to a boil. Add the broccoli, cover, and simmer for 3 minutes. Drain and remove the broccoli from the pan.

2 Add the olive oil, butter, and garlic to the skillet; cook and stir for 3 minutes over medium heat. Add the broccoli, stirring to coat with the oil. Season with the salt and pepper. Cook only until the broccoli is heated through.

3 Transfer the broccoli to a serving dish and garnish with shaved Parmesan cheese.

Makes 2 to 4 servings

¼ cup water

2 cups broccoli florets (about 1 pound)

2 tablespoons extra virgin olive oil

1 tablespoon unsalted butter

2 cloves garlic, finely chopped

¼ teaspoon kosher salt

¼ teaspoon ground white pepper

¼ pound Parmesan cheese, shaved with a vegetable peeler

Savory Rice

1 cup uncooked white long-grain rice

2 cups low-sodium beef broth

4 tablespoons unsalted butter

½ teaspoon salt

½ teaspoon ground white pepper

1 In a medium saucepan, bring the beef broth to a rapid boil over high heat. Add the rice, butter, salt, and pepper. Reduce heat to low and cover tightly.

2 Simmer until the liquid is absorbed and the rice is tender, 20 to 25 minutes. Remove from heat and let stand, covered, for 5 minutes.

3 Fluff the rice with a fork and serve hot.

Makes 2 to 4 servings

Easy Strawberry Shortcake

*W*hipped topping and strawberries—what more do you need to complete a Grown 'n' Sexy evening?

Place one slice of cake on each plate. Cover cake slices with strawberries and their juice and the whipped topping. Top with another slice of cake and cover with more strawberries and whipped topping. Garnish each serving with one whole strawberry and serve immediately.

Makes 4 servings

One 10- to 12-ounce storebought pound cake, cut into 8 slices

One 16-ounce container frozen sweetened sliced strawberries, thawed

One 8-ounce container frozen whipped topping, thawed (recommended: Cool Whip)

4 whole fresh strawberries, for garnish

Fettuccine Alfredo with Shrimp

8 ounces fettuccine

8 tablespoons unsalted butter

15 medium shrimp, peeled and deveined

⅛ teaspoon garlic powder

½ teaspoon salt

¼ teaspoon ground black pepper

1½ cups heavy cream

1 cup freshly grated Parmesan cheese, plus extra for serving

*t*his dish is so simple, you will wonder how it could possibly taste so good!

1 Bring a large pot of lightly salted water to a boil. Stir in the fettuccine and cook according to package directions for al dente. Drain and set aside.

2 Meanwhile, in a large saucepan over medium heat, melt the butter. Add the shrimp and season with garlic powder, salt, and pepper; cook and stir until shrimp turn pink throughout, 1 to 2 minutes.

3 Lower the heat and stir in the cream. Add the Parmesan and stir constantly until the cheese melts and the sauce thickens.

4 Transfer pasta to a serving dish, and cover with the shrimp Alfredo sauce. Toss to coat pasta thoroughly with the sauce and top with more grated Parmesan. Serve immediately.

Makes 4 servings

Herb-Crusted Sirloin

Succulent and hearty sirloin steak topped with a crisp and garlicky herb crust. Serve with Roasted Garlic Fingerling Potatoes (following page) to create another perfect date meal!

1 Preheat the broiler to 400°F.

2 Combine the garlic, parsley, bread crumbs, butter, salt, and pepper for the herb crust; blend well and set aside.

3 Season the steaks with additional salt and pepper. In a small bowl, combine the garlic and vegetable oil; rub into both sides of each steak.

4 Heat a grill pan over medium-high heat. Place the steaks on the grill pan and cook undisturbed for 2 minutes. Flip the steaks and cook the other side for 8 to 9 minutes for medium well.

5 Remove the pan from the heat. Spoon the herb crust, pressing down lightly, onto the top well side of each steak. Place the grill pan under the broiler and broil the steaks just until the crust is golden brown and crisp, 2 to 3 minutes.

6 Remove and allow steaks to rest for 3 minutes before serving.

Makes 2 to 4 servings

Herb Crust

1 clove garlic, minced

1 teaspoon chopped fresh flat-leaf parsley

¼ cup dry bread crumbs

4 tablespoons unsalted butter, melted

¼ teaspoon salt

¼ teaspoon ground black pepper

Sirloin

4 sirloin steaks (4 ounces each)

1½ teaspoons salt

½ teaspoon ground black pepper

1 clove garlic, minced

¼ cup vegetable oil

Roasted Garlic Fingerling Potatoes

1 pound unpeeled fingerling
potatoes, washed and scrubbed

3 tablespoons unsalted butter

2 cloves garlic, minced

2 teaspoons chopped shallots
(1 small shallot)

1 teaspoon salt

½ teaspoon ground black pepper

2 teaspoons chopped fresh flat-leaf
parsley

*m*y man is the true definition of a "meat and potatoes" type of guy . . . and these delicious potatoes don't disappoint! —*Jeniece*

1 Preheat oven to 425°F. Place the potatoes in a roasting pan and poke all over with a fork.

2 In a small saucepan, melt the butter over medium-low heat. Add the garlic and shallots and cook and stir until the garlic is fragrant, about 1 minute. Pour the butter mixture over the potatoes; season with salt and pepper, and toss to coat.

3 Place in the oven and roast, tossing every 15 minutes, until fork tender and crisp, about 30 minutes. Remove from oven and sprinkle with parsley just before serving.

Makes 2 to 4 servings

Homemade Vanilla Ice Cream with Brown Sugar Peaches

Okay, I know you are probably looking at this book like, "Are they crazy?" Relax and walk with us. How impressive would it be to have someone actually make you a batch of ice cream—in this millennium? You know: very impressive. So, get out that ice cream machine that you received as a housewarming gift and let's show this man that this is not a game!

1 Pour the cream into a large, heavy-bottomed saucepan. Split open the vanilla bean lengthwise and scrape the seeds into the cream. Add the entire vanilla bean to the cream. Over medium heat, bring almost to a boil, then remove from the heat and let the flavors infuse for 30 minutes.

2 Meanwhile, in a large bowl, whisk together the egg yolks and sugar until pale and the mixture leaves a trail when the whisk is lifted. Remove the vanilla bean from the cream mixture and slowly add the cream to the egg mixture, stirring constantly with a wooden spoon.

3 Pour the cream and egg mixture through a mesh strainer into a clean, large, heavy-bottomed sauce pan or a double boiler. Cook over low heat for 10 to 15 minutes, stirring constantly with a wooden spoon, until the mixture thickens enough to coat the back of the spoon. Do not let the mixture boil.

4 Remove the custard from the heat and let cool in the refrigerator for at least 1 hour, stirring every 15 minutes to prevent a skin from forming.

5 Using an ice cream machine, churn the custard following the manufacturer's instructions. Once set, spoon ice cream into a freezer-proof container and place in the freezer until ready to serve.

6 To make the brown sugar peaches, in a large, heavy-bottomed skillet over medium heat, melt the butter. Add the brown sugar and cinnamon and cook, stirring often, until sugar begins to dissolve.

7 Add the peaches; cook and stir until peaches are tender and sauce begins to thicken, about 5 minutes.

Homemade Vanilla Ice Cream

2½ cups heavy cream

1 vanilla bean

4 large egg yolks

½ cup confectioners' sugar

Brown Sugar Peaches

4 tablespoons unsalted butter

6 packed tablespoons light brown sugar

¾ teaspoon ground cinnamon

2 cups frozen peaches, thawed

2 teaspoons vanilla extract

8 Remove skillet from heat and stir in the vanilla extract. Spoon peaches and sauce over ice cream.

Makes 4 to 6 servings

The Morning After

The Cops Came Knocking! Menu
Buttermilk Waffles and Crisp Bacon
Veggie and Cheese Omelet
Freshly Squeezed Orange Juice

Let's Do It Again! Menu
Cinnamon French Toast
Scrambled Cheese Eggs
Home-Fried Potatoes and Sage Sausage

Good Morning, Sunshine! Menu
Salmon Cakes
Cheddar Cheese Grits
Toast with Apple Butter Spread

*t*he dinner was a success; now it's time to send him on his way completely turned out. Okay, we are assuming that he stayed the night. If you set it off the way you should have, he is probably curled up in the fetal position on your lavender-scented sheets right now.

So here it is, the morning after, and you want to fix him breakfast. Now, before you whip out the eggs and bacon, ask yourself . . . what type of breakfast did his performance warrant? Was it a cornflakes and milk type of performance? Was it a protein shake and yogurt type of performance? If you're lucky it was none of those things and we can skip straight to the omelet, waffles, and homemade muffin type of performance. All jokes aside, if he was privileged enough to get past the bedroom doors and stay the night, make sure you send him off in pure Get 'Em Girls' fashion, with wonderful memories and a full stomach.

Buttermilk Waffles and Crisp Bacon

*Y*ou are sure to impress him with this breakfast dish. Add some Freshly Squeezed Orange Juice (page 69) to the menu, and don't be surprised if he sticks around for lunch.

1 Preheat a waffle iron and lightly spray with nonstick cooking spray.

2 In a large bowl, sift together the flour, baking powder, baking soda, salt, and sugar.

3 In a small bowl, whisk the egg, buttermilk, and melted butter until combined.

4 Add the buttermilk mixture to the flour mixture and stir until smooth.

5 Prepare the bacon according to the package instructions. Drain the excess grease on a paper towel–lined platter before serving.

6 Pour the batter into the hot waffle iron, being careful not to overfill the iron and cook until golden brown and lightly crisp. Remove and serve immediately, topped with a pat of butter if desired, and warm maple syrup.

Makes 2 servings

1 cup all-purpose flour

1 teaspoon baking powder

¼ teaspoon baking soda

¼ teaspoon salt

¼ teaspoon sugar

1 large egg

1 cup buttermilk

4 tablespoons unsalted butter, melted

6 thick slices bacon (pork or turkey)

Butter, for serving (optional)

Warm maple syrup, for serving

Veggie and Cheese Omelet

3 large eggs

2 tablespoons heavy cream

⅛ teaspoon salt

⅛ teaspoon ground white pepper

1 tablespoon unsalted butter

1 tablespoon diced green bell pepper

1 tablespoon diced red bell pepper

1 tablespoon diced onion

¼ cup grated Cheddar cheese

*t*he perfect protein food to get him up and going—again and again!

1 In a small bowl, whisk the eggs, heavy cream, salt, and white pepper until frothy.

2 Heat a nonstick omelet pan over medium heat; add the butter to the pan, swirling to melt and coat. Add the peppers and onions; cook and stir until tender, about 2 minutes.

3 Pour the egg mixture into the pan. Using a silicone spatula, pull the cooked egg away from the pan and allow the raw egg to run onto the hot part of the pan. When almost set, sprinkle with 3 tablespoons of the Cheddar cheese.

4 Cook about 10 seconds longer and use the silicone spatula to fold the omelet in half. Top with the remaining tablespoon of cheese and carefully slide the omelet out of the pan and onto a plate.

Makes 1 serving

Freshly Squeezed Orange Juice

1 Roll the oranges against a hard surface to soften. Cut into halves and remove seeds. With a paring knife, carefully cut around the edge of the orange half, slightly separating the fruit and peel.

2 Grip each orange half tightly and squeeze directly into a glass or pitcher until liquid is no longer produced.

3 For less pulp, pour juice through a fine strainer before serving.

Makes 2 four-ounce servings

4 navel oranges

Cinnamon French Toast

½ cup pure maple syrup

5 tablespoons unsalted butter

2 teaspoons ground cinnamon

3 large eggs

1 cup heavy cream

½ teaspoon vanilla extract

⅛ teaspoon ground nutmeg

4 brioche bread slices, 1 inch thick

*t*hick and delicious, this is what French toast is supposed to taste like.

1 Bring the maple syrup, 1 tablespoon of the butter, and 1 teaspoon of the cinnamon to a boil in a small saucepan over medium heat. Boil for 2 minutes and remove from heat.

2 Whisk the eggs, heavy cream, vanilla, nutmeg, 3 tablespoons of the syrup mixture, and the remaining 1 teaspoon cinnamon in a bowl. Place the bread in a large baking dish. Pour the egg mixture over the bread, turning to coat. Pierce the bread with a fork. Let stand for 3 minutes.

3 Melt 2 tablespoons of the butter in a large heavy-bottomed skillet over medium heat. Add the bread and cook until the edges are slightly crisp and golden brown, 2 to 3 minutes. Add the remaining 2 tablespoons of butter to skillet. Turn over bread and cook until brown, 2 to 3 minutes. Transfer to plates and serve with the remaining syrup mixture.

Makes 2 servings

Scrambled Cheese Eggs

*t*hese moist and cheesy eggs will melt in his mouth.

1 Melt the butter in a large heavy nonstick skillet over medium heat. In a small bowl, briskly whisk together the eggs, salt, pepper, and water. Pour the egg mixture into the skillet.

2 Reduce the heat to low, and gently stir the egg mixture. Stir in the Cheddar and continue stirring until desired texture is achieved. Eggs will thicken and dry out very quickly toward the end, so be careful to remove from the heat promptly if you like your eggs soft and moist.

Makes 2 servings

3 tablespoons unsalted butter

5 large eggs

½ teaspoon salt

½ teaspoon ground white pepper

2 tablespoons water

½ cup grated Cheddar cheese

Home-Fried Potatoes and Sage Sausage

Home-Fried Potatoes

2 tablespoons olive oil

2 tablespoons butter

1 medium onion, chopped

4 large Russet potatoes, peeled and sliced ¼ inch thick

½ teaspoon water

1 teaspoon Get 'Em Girls' Essential Seasoning (page 29)

⅛ teaspoon garlic powder

½ teaspoon black pepper

Sage Sausage

1½ pounds sweet sage sausage

*C*hunky potatoes and caramelized onions, seasoned to perfection.

1 Heat the olive oil and butter in a large skillet over medium heat. Add the onions and cook until soft and browned, 10 to 15 minutes. Add the potatoes, water, Seasoning, garlic powder, and black pepper. Cover with a lid.

2 Cook for 8 to 10 minutes and flip once with a slotted spatula to brown the other side. Be sure to turn only once to prevent breaking up the potatoes. Continue to cook until the potatoes are fork tender, about 5 minutes.

3 Meanwhile, prepare the sage sausage according to package instructions. Slice into four 1-inch pieces and drain excess grease on a paper towel–lined plate.

4 Serve immediately.

Makes 4 servings

Salmon Cakes

*t*hese delicious pan-fried salmon cakes are easy to prepare and even easier to devour, especially with a hot serving of Cheddar Cheese Grits (following page).

1 Mix the flour and bread crumbs in a medium bowl. In a separate bowl, combine the salmon, egg, onion, Seasoning, black pepper, and ¼ cup of the flour mixture. Mix well and form into patties. Dust each cake with remaining flour mixture.

2 Heat the vegetable oil in a medium heavy skillet over medium heat. Fry the cakes until golden brown, 2 to 3 minutes on each side. Drain on a paper towel–lined platter and serve immediately.

Makes 2 to 4 servings

¼ **cup all-purpose flour**

¼ **cup dried bread crumbs**

One 14.75-ounce can pink salmon, flaked and deboned

1 large egg, beaten

2 tablespoons chopped yellow onion

½ **teaspoon Get 'Em Girls' Essential Seasoning (page 29)**

¼ **teaspoon ground black pepper**

½ **cup vegetable oil**

Cheddar Cheese Grits

2 cups water

1¼ cups milk

1 teaspoon salt, plus more to taste

1 cup quick-cooking grits (not instant)

8 tablespoons butter

½ cup shredded Cheddar cheese

Ground black pepper

1 In a small pot, bring the water, milk, and salt to a boil. Slowly stir in grits. Stir continuously until grits are mixed well. Let the pot return to a boil, cover with a tight-fitting lid and reduce the temperature to low.

2 Simmer for approximately 30 minutes, stirring occasionally. Add more water if necessary. Once grits have a smooth and creamy consistency, remove from heat.

3 Stir in 4 tablespoons of the butter and the Cheddar. Stir until the cheese is melted and incorporated thoroughly. Season to taste with additional salt and pepper. Serve hot with the remaining butter.

Makes 4 servings

Toast with Apple Butter Spread

Show him your creative skills by whipping up this smooth and delightful spread. Who knew toast could taste so good? Unused apple butter spread can be stored in the refrigerator for up to two weeks.

1 Heat a large grill pan over medium-high heat and toast the brioche slices, turning once.

2 Spread 1½ teaspoons of butter on one side of each slice and set aside.

3 For the apple butter spread: whip the cream cheese and apple butter together in a medium bowl.

4 Spread on toast and serve immediately. Refrigerate remaining apple butter spread for up to 7 days.

Makes 4 servings

4 slices brioche bread, about 1 inch thick

2 tablespoons unsalted butter, room temperature

One 8-ounce package cream cheese, room temperature

1 cup apple butter

Simple Southern-Fried Chicken

(Recipe on page 27)

Jumpin' Jumpin' Jambalaya

(Recipe on page 119)

Vegetable Fried Rice and Shrimp Egg Rolls

(Recipes on pages 94 and 92)

Salmon with Brown Sugar Glaze,
Sautéed Garlic Asparagus, and Kiss o' Honey Potatoes
(Recipes on pages 51–53)

Homemade Tortilla Chips

(Recipe on page 139)

Buttermilk Waffles and Crisp Bacon
(Recipe on page 67)

Homemade Vanilla Ice Cream with Brown Sugar Peaches
(Recipe on page 63)

Yes-They're-Good-for-You Oatmeal Cookies

(Recipe on page 181)

A Trip for Two

Yo Quiero Papi Menu

Broiled Chicken

Spanish Yellow Rice

Spanish-Style Paella

Creamed Spinach

Fried Sweet Plantains (*Maduros*)

Tres Leches (Three Milks) Cake

Get 'Em Girls' Sangria

Island Hoppin' Menu

Coconut Shrimp with Honey-Orange Dipping Sauce

Steamed Red Snapper

Curried Chicken

Goongo Peas and Rice

Steamed Callaloo

Coconut Cream Parfait

Asian Menu

Shrimp Egg Rolls

Hoisin-Glazed Pork Chops

Vegetable Fried Rice

Flirty Fortune Cookies

Mint Iced Green Tea

*i*t is twenty degrees outside on a snowy evening and the last thing you want to do is go out for dinner and a movie in this weather. How about inviting him over for some fun, food, and fantasies. Just imagine snow and sleet outside and Caribbean grooves inside.

First and foremost, you have to set the stage for the evening. If it is a Caribbean theme you're going for, pick up a Bob Marley greatest hits CD to set the mood for the evening. Stop at your local party store and pick up some tropical-themed props (i.e., raffia table skirts, coconut cups, or island-inspired tableware and place settings.

For a little Latin flair, pop in some Novalima or Carlos Santana to set the mood, whip up a pitcher of delicious Sangria with glasses to match and pick up some inexpensive and practical serving pieces that will set the tone and create the atmosphere you want to evoke.

To create an Asian-inspired evening, how about purchasing some bamboo mats, chopsticks, and theme-centered place settings for two? For added effect, pick up a sexy kimono to wear for the evening.

Just the fact that you were inventive and thoughtful enough to create this type of experience for him will leave a lasting impression, and once he tastes the delicious meal you've cooked, he'll be wondering which exotic "trip" you two are going on next. Hey, just think . . . he might plan something special on his own . . . well, you never know!

Broiled Chicken

*t*his is a simple and easy dish that is full of Latin flavor. Served with Spanish Yellow Rice (following page), this is sure to be a winner.

1 Rinse and clean the chicken, pat dry, and place in a resealable plastic bag. Mix the olive oil, vinegar, salt, pepper, oregano, and garlic in a bowl. Pour over the chicken. Close the bag, releasing any air, and rub the seasoning thoroughly into chicken parts. Refrigerate for 6 hours or preferably overnight.

2 When ready to cook, preheat the broiler to high.

3 Remove the chicken from the bag and discard the remaining marinade. Broil the chicken in a pan, turning once and basting frequently with pan juices until juices run clear and no pink shows, about 30 minutes. Serve immediately.

Makes 4 servings

One 3-pound chicken, cut into 8 pieces

½ cup olive oil

1½ tablespoons distilled white vinegar

1 teaspoon salt

1 teaspoon ground black pepper

1 teaspoon dried oregano

2 cloves garlic, crushed

Spanish Yellow Rice

2 tablespoons extra virgin olive oil

½ cup chopped Spanish onion

¼ cup chopped green bell pepper

½ cup drained diced tomatoes

1 packet Sazón with coriander and annatto

½ teaspoon salt

¼ teaspoon ground black pepper

2 cups low-sodium chicken broth

1 cup long-grain white or basmati rice

1 Heat the olive oil in a medium saucepan over medium heat. Add the onion and green pepper; cook and stir until onion is translucent. Stir in the tomatoes, Sazón, salt, and pepper. Continue to cook for 1 minute.

2 Add the chicken broth and bring to a boil. Stir in rice and bring to a second boil.

3 Cover with a tight-fitting lid and reduce heat to low. Simmer until broth is absorbed and rice is tender, 20 to 25 minutes.

Makes 4 servings

Spanish-Style Paella

a couple of years ago while on a Caribbean cruise I ate some of the best paella I ever had in my life. As soon as I hit land, I immediately ran to my kitchen and re-created this savory dish. —*Jeniece*

1 Clean and rinse chicken under cold water and pat dry. In a small bowl, combine the oregano, paprika, turmeric, salt, and pepper. Rub the spice mixture all over the chicken pieces and cover with plastic wrap. Let marinate in the refrigerator for 30 minutes.

2 Heat the olive oil in a large heavy-bottomed skillet over medium-high heat. Add the chicken, skin side down, and brown on all sides. Add the chorizo sausages and continue to cook for 5 to 7 minutes. Remove the chicken and sausage to a platter and set aside.

3 Add the onion, bell pepper, tomatoes, and garlic to the skillet. Lower the heat to medium and cook, stirring occasionally until the mixture begins to brown. Season with salt and pepper.

4 Stir in the rice and saffron. Add the water and mix well. Cover and simmer on low until liquid is absorbed, about 15 minutes.

5 Tuck the chicken, chorizo, shrimp, and lobster (if using) into the paella mixture. Cover and let simmer for 10 to 15 minutes.

6 Scatter the peas on top and cook uncovered until the paella is fluffy and moist, about 5 minutes. Let sit for 5 minutes and garnish with parsley leaves.

Makes 8 servings

1½ pounds cut-up chicken (8 pieces)

1 teaspoon dried oregano

1½ tablespoons sweet paprika

1 teaspoon turmeric

½ teaspoon salt, plus more to taste

½ teaspoon ground black pepper, plus more to taste

3 tablespoons extra virgin olive oil

2 Spanish-style chorizo sausages, sliced into ¼-inch rounds

1 Spanish onion, diced

1 cup seeded and chopped green bell pepper

One 14.5- to 16-ounce can whole tomatoes (about 2 cups), drained and hand crushed

3 cloves garlic, crushed

1 cup long-grain white rice

1 teaspoon saffron threads

2 cups water

8 extra large shrimp, peeled and deveined

1 shelled lobster tail, thawed if frozen (optional)

½ cup frozen sweet peas, thawed

Fresh flat-leaf parsley, for garnish

Creamed Spinach

Two 10-ounce packages frozen chopped spinach, thawed

¼ teaspoon salt

2 tablespoons unsalted butter

1 tablespoon all-purpose flour

¾ cup milk

¼ teaspoon ground black pepper

⅛ teaspoon freshly grated nutmeg

¼ cup freshly grated Parmesan cheese (optional)

*f*ast and easy to prepare, frozen spinach is added to a mixture of milk, butter, and flour.

1 Place the spinach in a colander over a medium bowl. Squeeze until all the liquid is out of spinach. Reserve ¼ cup of spinach liquid and set aside.

2 In a medium saucepan over medium heat, combine the spinach, reserved spinach liquid, and salt. Cook and stir for 2 minutes. Drain and set aside.

3 Melt the butter in a separate medium saucepan over medium-low heat. Add the flour to the butter and whisk until smooth. Slowly add the milk and whisk briskly until mixture starts to thicken.

4 Add the spinach, black pepper, nutmeg, and Parmesan, if using. Stir to combine and serve immediately.

Makes 4 servings

Fried Sweet Plantains (*Maduros*)

3 very ripe yellow plantains

¼ cup vegetable oil

1 Peel the plantains and cut into diagonal slices, about ½ inch thick and 3 inches long.

2 Heat the vegetable oil in a medium skillet over medium-low heat. Fry the plantain slices in the oil until slightly browned and tender, about 3 minutes. Carefully flip plantains with a slotted spatula and cook until slightly browned. Remove from heat and serve immediately.

Makes 2 to 4 servings

Tres Leches (Three Milks) Cake

Cake Mix Package

One 18.25-ounce package yellow cake mix with pudding added

1¼ cups water

⅓ cup vegetable oil

3 large eggs

1 pint heavy cream

One 12-ounce can evaporated milk

One 14-ounce can sweetened condensed milk

One 8-ounce container frozen whipped topping, thawed

¼ cup sweetened flaked coconut (optional)

*C*hill to almost frozen—this ice cream cake–like dessert will cool down all the heat created during dinner . . . that is, if you're trying to cool it down!

1 Prepare the cake according to the package directions for a 13 x 9-inch cake pan. Let cool completely in the pan.

2 Meanwhile, in a large bowl, combine the heavy cream with the evaporated and condensed milks. Mix well and set aside.

3 Poke holes all over cake with a fork and pour the milk mixture over cake. Cover with plastic wrap and refrigerate for 4 hours.

4 Remove from the refrigerator and cover with the whipped topping. Sprinkle with the coconut, if desired, and serve immediately.

Makes 6 to 8 servings

Get 'Em Girls' Sangria

*a*dd a little sizzle to your evening with our delicious and potent drink. Sip slowly and enjoy!

1 Pour the wine and schnapps into a large pitcher. Stir in the peaches, orange and apple wedges. Add the sugar to the pitcher and stir to dissolve. Chill the mixture for 1 hour.

2 Add the ginger ale just before serving.

Makes 6 to 8 servings

1 750ml bottle sweet white wine, chilled (recommended: Vision Cellars Riesling)

½ cup peach schnapps (recommended: DeKuyper's)

2 cups frozen sliced peaches

1 orange, cut into 6 wedges

1 Granny Smith apple, cut into 6 wedges and cored

¼ cup sugar

2 cups ginger ale

Coconut Shrimp with Honey-Orange Dipping Sauce

½ cup sweetened flaked coconut

½ cup panko bread crumbs

Salt and ground black pepper

½ cup all-purpose flour

2 large eggs, beaten

Vegetable oil, for frying

12 large shrimp, peeled and deveined

*S*erve as a main dish or appetizer.

1 Combine the coconut and bread crumbs in a large bowl. Season to taste with salt and pepper. Place the flour and eggs in 2 separate bowls.

2 In a large Dutch oven, heat about 3 inches of vegetable oil to 350°F.

3 Coat the shrimp in the flour, shaking off any excess. Follow by dipping the shrimp in the egg mixture and then coating thoroughly with the coconut mixture.

4 In batches, fry the shrimp until golden brown and cooked through, 3 to 4 minutes per batch. Remove from the oil with a slotted spoon and drain on a paper towel–lined platter. Serve immediately.

Makes 2 to 4 servings

½ cup orange marmalade

¼ cup Dijon mustard

¼ cup honey

Hot pepper sauce (optional)

Honey-Orange Dipping Sauce

In a small bowl, combine all of the ingredients. Mix well and serve alongside Coconut Shrimp.

Makes about 1 cup

Steamed Red Snapper

*i*n our best West Indian accent . . . Serve your mon dis authentic island dish and everything will be irie!

1 Season the fish with 1 teaspoon salt and 1 teaspoon black pepper.

2 Melt the butter in a large skillet over medium heat. Add the fish, onion, garlic, carrot, tomato, bell pepper, thyme, and water. Cook, stirring occasionally, for 5 minutes, making sure not to break up fish.

3 Reduce heat to low, cover, and steam for 10 minutes. Add cabbage, season with remaining salt and black pepper, cover, and steam for an additional 5 minutes.

4 Transfer the fish to a platter and serve immediately with vegetables on top.

Makes 4 servings

4 red snapper fillets, about 1 pound total

2 teaspoons kosher salt

1½ teaspoons ground black pepper

3 tablespoons unsalted butter

1 small onion, thinly sliced into half moons

1 clove garlic, chopped

1 large carrot, peeled and thinly sliced diagonally

1 small tomato, chopped

1 small green bell pepper, seeded and sliced into ½-inch strips

2 sprigs fresh thyme

⅓ cup water

4 cups coarsely chopped green cabbage

Curried Chicken

One (2- to 2½-pound) fryer chicken, cut into 8 pieces

1 cup lemon or lime juice

1 large onion, chopped

4 small Russet potatoes, peeled and cubed

3 tablespoons curry powder

1½ teaspoons dried thyme

2 teaspoons kosher salt

1 teaspoon ground black pepper

2 cloves garlic, chopped

½ teaspoon sugar

3 tablespoons vegetable oil

1 sprig fresh thyme

¼ cup chicken stock

1 Clean and rinse chicken under cold water. Place in a large bowl and add lemon or lime juice; let sit for 1 minute, rinse well with cold water, and pat dry.

2 In a separate large bowl, combine the onions, potatoes, 2 tablespoons of the curry powder, the dried thyme, salt, black pepper, garlic, and sugar. Mix well and let sit for 10 minutes to allow flavors to combine. Add the chicken and mix well. Cover with plastic wrap and refrigerate for 20 to 30 minutes.

3 Heat the vegetable oil in a large skillet over medium heat. Stir the remaining tablespoon of curry powder and the fresh thyme into the vegetable oil. Carefully add the chicken pieces and brown on all sides, about 10 minutes.

4 Add the chicken stock and vegetables and cover tightly. Reduce heat to low and simmer until chicken is tender and shows no sign of pink, about 25 minutes. Remove from heat and serve immediately.

Makes 6 to 8 servings

Goongo Peas and Rice

*P*eas and rice sweetened with coconut milk is a traditional dish throughout the Caribbean. Serve with iron-rich Steamed Callaloo (following page) for an authentic Caribbean dining experience. If you can't find goongo peas, use pigeon peas.

1 Bring the water to boil in a large saucepan. Add the peas, scallion, onion, thyme, salt, pepper, garlic, and coconut milk. Bring to a second boil and cook for 15 minutes.

2 Stir in the rice; lower heat, cover, and steam for 25 minutes. Remove from heat and serve immediately.

Makes 6 to 8 servings

4 cups water

One 19-ounce can goongo peas, rinsed and drained

1 scallion, white and green parts, chopped

1 small onion, chopped

2 sprigs fresh thyme, chopped

2 teaspoons salt

1 teaspoon ground black pepper

1 clove garlic, chopped

2 cups coconut milk

3 cups uncooked white rice

Steamed Callaloo

1 tablespoon unsalted butter

1 medium onion, thinly sliced

2 cups washed and chopped fresh callaloo (or kale as a substitute)

¼ cup water

1 teaspoon salt

½ teaspoon ground black pepper

Melt the butter in a large saucepan over medium heat. Add the onion and cook until translucent, about 5 minutes. Stir in the callaloo and water. Lower the heat, cover the saucepan, and simmer until callaloo is tender, 15 to 20 minutes. Season with salt and pepper. Remove from heat and serve immediately.

Makes 2 to 4 servings

Coconut Cream Parfait

*S*mooth custard layered with sweet coconut and crunchy golden graham crackers.

1 In a large bowl, whisk together the pudding mix and milk. Add the vanilla extract and continue to whisk the mixture until it thickens. Fold ¾ cup of coconut and half of the whipped topping into the pudding. Cover with plastic wrap and refrigerate until ready to serve.

2 Sprinkle 1 tablespoon of the graham cracker crumbs into each of four martini glasses or dessert bowls. Spoon the pudding mixture over the crumbs. Garnish with more graham cracker crumbs and the remaining coconut. Serve immediately.

Makes 4 servings

One 5-ounce package instant vanilla pudding mix

1½ cups milk

½ teaspoon vanilla extract

1 cup sweetened flaked coconut

One 8-ounce container frozen whipped topping, thawed

¼ cup graham cracker crumbs

Shrimp Egg Rolls

2 tablespoons peanut or vegetable oil

4 cups shredded green cabbage

3 scallions, white and green parts, thinly sliced

½ cup fresh bean sprouts

1 tablespoon soy sauce

1 teaspoon light brown sugar

1 cup chopped cooked shrimp

One 8-ounce package egg roll skins

1 large egg, beaten

Vegetable oil, for frying

Prepared Chinese mustard, for serving (optional)

Sweet-and-sour sauce, for serving (optional)

*W*hy order take-out when you can make it yourself?

1 Heat the peanut oil in a large wok or skillet over medium-high heat. Add the cabbage, scallions, and bean sprouts, and toss with oil to coat. Raise the heat to high and stir-fry until the cabbage gets limp, about 3 minutes.

2 Add the soy sauce, brown sugar, and shrimp. Cook and stir until heated through, about 1 minute. Transfer to a bowl with a slotted spoon and allow to cool completely.

3 Place the egg roll wrappers on a flat work surface, with a corner facing you. Fill the egg roll wrappers with about ¼ cup of filling per egg roll.

4 To close, fold the tip facing you over the filling toward the center. Lightly brush the side tips of the wrapper with some of the beaten egg, and then fold them into the center, overlapping them if necessary.

5 Brush the tip farthest from you with a little of the beaten egg and fold toward you to seal the egg roll. Repeat with the remaining wrappers and filling. You should have enough filling for 6 to 8 egg rolls.

6 While you are rolling the egg rolls, heat the vegetable oil in a large heavy-bottomed skillet to 350°F. Carefully add 2 egg rolls to the vegetable oil and fry, turning frequently with tongs, until golden brown, 4 to 5 minutes. Repeat with the remaining egg rolls. Place egg rolls on a paper towel–lined plate to absorb the oil. Serve immediately with store-bought Chinese mustard or sweet-and-sour sauce.

Makes 6 to 8 servings

Hoisin-Glazed Pork Chops

*C*hinese barbecue sauce lightly brushed over thick, juicy chops.

1 Preheat the oven to 400°F.

2 In a large bowl, whisk together the scallions, hoisin sauce, oyster sauce, mustard, ginger, and honey. Add the pork chops to the bowl and coat with the sauce.

3 Arrange the pork chops in a shallow baking dish. Lightly brush the pork chops with additional sauce. Roast uncovered for 15 to 20 minutes.

4 Turn on the broiler and place the pork chops 5 to 6 inches from heat. Cook until the top is slightly caramelized, 2 to 5 minutes. Let stand uncovered for 5 minutes. Serve immediately with the pan juices.

Makes 4 servings

1 bunch scallions, trimmed and sliced into 2-inch pieces

2 tablespoons plus 1½ teaspoons hoisin sauce

3 tablespoons oyster sauce

1 tablespoon plus 1½ teaspoons Dijon mustard

¼ teaspoon finely grated fresh ginger

2 tablespoons honey

4 center-cut pork chops, about 1 inch thick

Vegetable Fried Rice

2 tablespoons vegetable oil

2 cups cooked long-grain white rice, chilled

1 cup frozen peas and carrots, thawed

1 teaspoon salt

2 large eggs, beaten

½ cup fresh bean sprouts

2 tablespoons scallions, thinly sliced

1 Heat a wok or large skillet over high heat. Add the vegetable oil and continue to heat until oil is almost smoking.

2 Add the rice; cook and stir for 1 minute. Add the peas and carrots and season with salt. Cook and stir for 5 minutes over high heat.

3 Stir in the beaten eggs and bean sprouts and continue to cook until the eggs have set, about 2 minutes. Remove from the heat and transfer to a serving bowl. Garnish with the scallions and serve immediately.

Makes 4 servings

Flirty Fortune Cookies

*i*magine his expression when he reads the sexy and suggestive fortunes you have created just for him.

1 Write or type flirtatious fortunes on pieces of paper that are 3½ inches long and ½ inch wide.

2 Preheat oven to 300°F. Grease 2 cookie sheets with nonstick cooking spray and set aside.

3 In a medium bowl, lightly beat the egg whites, vanilla and almond extracts, and vegetable oil until frothy. In a separate bowl, sift together the flour, cornstarch, salt, and sugar.

4 Stir the water into the flour mixture. Add the flour mixture into the egg white mixture and stir until smooth.

5 Place 1 tablespoon of batter onto one of the prepared baking sheets. Gently tilt the baking sheet back and forth so that the batter forms a 4-inch circle.

6 Bake until the outer ½ inch of the cookie turns golden brown and is easy to lift from the baking sheet with a small off-set spatula, 12 to 14 minutes.

7 Working quickly, remove the cookie with the spatula and flip it over onto a clean, flat work surface or into your hand. Place a fortune in the middle of the cookie and quickly fold in half. Gently pull the edges of the halved cookie downward over the rim of a glass.

8 Place the finished cookie in the cup of a muffin tin so that it keeps its shape. Continue with the rest of the cookies, using the unused baking sheet while the other cools completely.

Makes 8 to 9 cookies

2 large egg whites

½ teaspoon vanilla extract

½ teaspoon almond extract

3 tablespoons vegetable oil

½ cup all-purpose flour

1½ teaspoons cornstarch

¼ teaspoon salt

½ cup sugar

1 tablespoon water

MAKE IT YOUR OWN

For chocolate-dipped fortune cookies, melt 8 ounces of semi-sweet chocolate and 1 tablespoon of vegetable shortening in a double boiler or a glass bowl over boiling water. Stir continually while melting, making sure not to get any water into the mixture. Dip the bottom of each cookie into the melted chocolate and place on a wax paper–lined cookie sheet. Refrigerate to harden.

Mint Iced Green Tea

6 cups water

½ cup fresh mint leaves, plus more
for garnish

6 green tea bags

¼ cup honey

¼ cup sugar

1 tablespoon fresh lemon juice

1 In a large saucepan over high heat, bring the water to a boil. Remove from heat and add the mint leaves and tea bags. Cover and let steep for 15 minutes.

2 Strain the tea into a 2-quart pitcher and add the honey, sugar, and lemon juice. Refrigerate until chilled.

3 Serve over ice cubes and garnish with additional mint leaves.

Makes about 6 one-cup servings

Soups and Salads for the Soul

Soups

Nancy's Goulash Stew

Bring Him Back! Chicken Soup

Creamy Tomato Soup with Grown-Up! Grilled Cheese

Dee's Split Pea Soup

Cajun Gumbo

Grandma's Hot Toddy

Salads

Egg Salad with Pita Wedges

Bacon and Blue Cheese Wedge Salad

Quick Side Salad

Chicken Salad

My mom cooked every day.
Every man looks for his mother when looking for a mate.
—Fred Monpremiere *Los Angeles, CA*

*h*e just called you to let you know he has the cold from hell: his nose is runny, his head is stuffy, and nothing he's taking is working. What he needs is some good old-fashioned homemade soup. How about whipping something up that will not only leave him feeling much better physically, but will having him wondering, "Where have you been all my life?"

Whether it's a pot of cold-remedy chicken soup or a light lunch date at his place, the recipes in this section are great as stand-alone dishes, or as quick additions to any meal you are cooking.

Make him say ahhhhhh . . .

*h*ere are some really sweet ideas to make him feel better and help pass the time while he's whining like a big baby and infecting your favorite down comforter with his nasty germs:

Board Games!

Break out the Scrabble and go easy on him—no triple word scores!

Flowers!

Contrary to what you may have heard, men can appreciate a delivery of beautiful flowers just as much as you can.

Man Movies!

Scarface, Reservoir Dogs, Gladiator, The Usual Suspects, and the like . . . suck it up!

Hot Chocolate

. . . with whipped cream, shaved chocolate, and marshmallows!

Childhood Candies!

Lemonheads, Boston Baked Beans, Now and Laters, or Mike and Ikes.

Nancy's Goulash Stew

2 pounds chuck steak, cut into ½-inch cubes

½ cup all-purpose flour, seasoned with salt and pepper

4 tablespoons unsalted butter

Two 28-ounce cans whole tomatoes, with their juice

3 medium Russet potatoes, peeled and cubed

2 cups beef broth

¼ cup paprika

Salt and ground black pepper

6 to 8 sourdough bread bowls, for serving

1 cup sour cream, for garnish

Fresh dill sprigs, chopped, for garnish

*g*reat advice and beauty tips are not the only two things Nancy is known for. She is also known for burning in the kitchen, and this stew is proof of that!

1 In a large bowl, toss the steak in the seasoned flour and set aside. Meanwhile, melt the butter in a Dutch oven or large pot over medium heat. Add the steak to the pot and brown on all sides.

2 Stir in the tomatoes, potatoes, beef broth, and paprika. Bring to a boil. Season to taste with salt and pepper.

3 Reduce the heat, cover, and simmer for 30 minutes, or until potatoes are tender. Serve in a crusty sourdough bread bowl. Garnish each with a dollop of sour cream and dill; serve immediately.

Makes 6 to 8 servings

Bring Him Back! Chicken Soup

When the nightcaps go from Chardonnay to NyQuil®, it's time to kick into Get 'Em Girls' mode and bring him back!

1 Wash the chicken under cold running water. Place in a large stockpot or Dutch oven with enough water to cover, about 2 quarts. Add the onion, garlic, bay leaves, bouillon cubes, thyme, salt, and pepper, and bring to a boil.

2 Reduce the heat to low and simmer, partially covered, until the chicken begins to pull away from the bone, about 1 hour. Remove any fat that has risen to the top of the stock with a skimmer or large spoon as the chicken cooked.

3 Remove the chicken from the stock and set aside until cool enough to handle. Remove and discard the bay leaves and onion. Pull the chicken meat off the bones, discarding the bones, skin, and any remaining fat. Chop the meat into bite-size pieces and set aside.

4 Bring stock back to a boil and add the carrots and celery. Reduce the heat to medium-low and simmer until the vegetables are tender, 15 to 20 minutes. Return the meat to the stock and season to taste with additional salt and pepper.

5 Add the rotini noodles and simmer until noodles are cooked through, 10 to 12 minutes. Remove from the heat and stir in the parsley. Serve immediately.

Makes 4 servings

One 3-pound chicken, cut up

1 large onion, quartered

1 clove garlic, minced

2 bay leaves

2 chicken bouillon cubes

1 sprig fresh thyme

1 teaspoon salt

½ teaspoon pepper

2 carrots, peeled and chopped

2 celery stalks, chopped

1½ cups uncooked rotini noodles

2 tablespoons chopped fresh flat-leaf parsley

Creamy Tomato Soup with Grown-Up! Grilled Cheese

1 cup diced onion

2 tablespoons unsalted butter

2 tablespoons all-purpose flour

1 teaspoon salt

1 teaspoon sugar

½ teaspoon chopped fresh basil

¼ teaspoon ground white pepper

2 cups warm milk

2 cups canned crushed tomatoes

⅛ teaspoon baking soda

*W*arm and soothing, this soup goes great with a Grilled Cheese sandwich.

1 In a Dutch oven over medium heat, cook and stir onions in the butter until translucent, about 5 minutes. Remove from the heat and stir in the flour, salt, sugar, basil, and white pepper.

2 Add ¾ cup of the warm milk and blend well. Gradually add the remaining milk, stirring constantly.

3 Heat the tomatoes in a separate pot over medium-high heat. Remove from heat and add the baking soda. Let the tomatoes stand for 3 minutes. Add to the white sauce. Serve immediately.

Makes 4 servings

TAKE NOTE

For smoother tomato soup, blend with an immersion stick blender right before serving.

---

4 ounces sliced Havarti cheese

One 8 x 6-inch piece focaccia, sliced in half horizontally

4 tablespoons butter, room temperature

Grown-Up! Grilled Cheese

1 Arrange the cheese on the bottom layer of the bread. Top with the other half of the bread and press firmly to seal. Brush both sides of the sandwich with butter. **2** Lightly butter a heavy skillet. Cook the sandwich over medium-high heat until the cheese is fully melted and the sandwich is golden brown on both sides, about 4 minutes per side. Slice diagonally and serve immediately.

Makes 2 servings

Dee's Split Pea Soup

*W*onderfully warming comfort food. Grab a blanket, two bowls, and some crusty bread, and make it a movie weekend.

1 Combine the peas, sausage, onion, and ham in a large stockpot. Cover with the water and bring to a boil.

2 Reduce heat to medium-low and simmer for 45 minutes, stirring occasionally, and adding more water if necessary.

3 Add the carrots and potatoes and continue simmering until vegetables are tender, 15 to 20 minutes. Season to taste with salt and pepper. Serve warm with crusty Italian bread.

Makes 6 servings

1½ cups dried split peas

One 16-ounce package Kielbasa sausage, chopped into ¼-inch cubes

1 small onion, chopped

½ pound ham steak, chopped into ¼-inch cubes

6 cups cold water, plus more as needed

1 cup peeled, chopped carrots, sliced thick

1 small Russet potato, peeled and diced

Salt and ground black pepper

Crusty Italian bread, for serving

Cajun Gumbo

6 cups water

One 2-pound chicken, cut up into 8 pieces

¼ cup plus 2 tablespoons vegetable oil

1 cup sliced okra

⅛ cup all-purpose flour

½ cup chopped onion

½ cup chopped celery

½ cup chopped green pepper

1 teaspoon salt

1 clove garlic, minced

½ teaspoon ground black pepper

½ teaspoon cayenne pepper

8 ounces andouille sausage, sliced thick

2 cups canned whole peeled tomatoes, with juice

2 bay leaves

1½ teaspoons filé powder (optional)

Cooked white rice, for serving

*a*dd a bit of the Bayou to your menu with this classic Cajun dish.

1 Combine the water and chicken in a large stockpot over high heat and bring to a boil. Reduce heat to low and simmer until the chicken begins to pull away from the bone, about 1 hour. Remove any fat that has risen to the top of the stock with a skimmer or large spoon as the chicken cooked.

2 Remove the chicken from the stock and set aside until cool enough to handle; reserve the chicken stock. Once cool, pull the chicken meat off the bones. Discard the bones, skin, and any remaining fat, and set aside.

3 Heat 2 tablespoons of the oil in a heavy skillet over medium heat. Add the okra; cook and stir until no longer sticky, about 20 minutes. Set aside.

4 To make the roux, stir flour and the remaining ¼ cup oil together in a large heavy saucepan or Dutch oven. Cook and stir over medium heat until deep golden brown, about 6 minutes.

5 Stir the onion, celery, green pepper, salt, garlic, black pepper, and cayenne into the roux. Cook and stir over medium heat, for 3 minutes.

6 Gradually add 3 cups of the reserved chicken stock, the okra, chicken, andouille sausage, tomatoes, and bay leaves, and bring to a boil. Cover partially and reduce heat to low, simmer until thickened, about 1 hour. Remove the bay leaves.

7 If desired, served with ¼ teaspoon of filé powder to stir into each serving. Serve immediately with white rice.

Makes 6 servings

Grandma's Hot Toddy

1 Place the tea bag and boiling water in a medium tea cup and let steep for 5 minutes.

2 Remove the tea bag and stir in the honey until completely dissolved. Mix in the brandy and serve with the lemon slice.

Makes 1 serving

1 orange pekoe tea bag

¾ cup boiling water

1 tablespoon honey

2 ounces brandy

1 slice lemon

Egg Salad with Pita Wedges

4 slices thick-cut bacon

6 large eggs

¼ cup mayonnaise

½ teaspoon salt

¼ teaspoon ground black pepper

⅛ teaspoon sweet paprika

2 whole-wheat pitas, cut into 4 wedges each

*i*nvite him to a nice picnic lunch in the park—or in your bed!

1 Prepare the bacon according to package directions. Drain, crumble, and set aside.

2 Place the eggs in a medium saucepan with enough cold water to cover and bring to a boil. Cover with a tight-fitting lid and remove from heat. Let the eggs stand in the hot water for 10 to 15 minutes. Remove from hot water and let cool before peeling. Chop coarsely and set aside in a large bowl.

3 Mix the mayonnaise, salt, pepper, and paprika into the eggs. Mash lightly with a fork. Serve with crumbled bacon sprinkled on top and pita wedges on the side.

Makes 2 servings

Bacon and Blue Cheese Wedge Salad

*t*asty enough for a light lunch and hearty enough for a light dinner—store the blue cheese dressing in an airtight jar and refrigerate for up to 3 days.

1 In a small bowl, combine the mayonnaise, lemon juice, ground black pepper, and hot pepper sauce. Add the blue cheese and stir until well blended. Refrigerate until ready to use.

2 In a large skillet, preferably cast iron, cook the bacon over medium-high heat until golden brown and beginning to crisp.

3 Arrange the lettuce on plates and drizzle with dressing. Using a slotted spoon, transfer warm bacon from the skillet onto the salads, dividing equally.

Makes 6 servings

1½ cups mayonnaise

4½ teaspoons lemon juice

1½ teaspoons ground black pepper

1 teaspoon hot pepper sauce

1 cup coarsely crumbled blue cheese

½ pound thick-cut bacon, cut into 1-inch pieces

1 large head iceberg lettuce, cut into 6 wedges

Quick Side Salad

One 10-ounce bag mixed salad greens, washed and thoroughly dried

½ cup peeled and shredded carrots

1 cup cherry tomatoes, cut in half

½ cup freshly grated Parmesan cheese

1 cup creamy Parmesan salad dressing

⅛ teaspoon ground black pepper

2 cups croutons

In a large salad bowl, combine the salad greens, carrots, tomatoes, Parmesan cheese and dressing, and black pepper, and toss gently. Top with the croutons and serve.

Makes 4 servings

Chicken Salad

*a*bsolutely delicious alone or on ciabatta bread.

1 Wash the chicken under cold running water. Place in a large stockpot or Dutch oven with enough water to cover, about 2 quarts. Add the yellow onion, celery stalk, salt, and ¼ teaspoon ground black pepper, and bring to a boil.

2 Reduce the heat to low and simmer until the chicken shows no sign of pink when pierced in the thickest part, about 20 minutes. Remove from heat and let cool in the liquid.

3 Once cool enough to handle, transfer the chicken to a platter, remove and discard the skin, bones, and any remaining fat. Strain the chicken stock through cheesecloth or a mesh strainer, discarding the onion and celery; reserve and refrigerate the chicken stock in an airtight jar for another use at a later date. Dice the chicken into ¾-inch pieces and place in a large bowl.

4 Add the eggs, diced celery, red onion, pickle relish, Seasoning, mayonnaise, the remaining ½ teaspoon black pepper, and the red pepper flakes, if using. Mix well. Cover with plastic wrap and refrigerate until ready to serve.

Makes 6 servings

One 3-pound chicken, cubed

1 small yellow onion, quartered

1 stalk celery

½ teaspoon kosher salt

¾ teaspoon ground black pepper

4 hard-cooked eggs, chopped (see note page 41)

¾ cup finely diced celery

½ cup finely diced red onion

½ cup sweet pickle relish

2 teaspoons Get 'Em Girls' Essential Seasoning (page 29)

1 cup mayonnaise

⅛ teaspoon crushed red pepper flakes (optional)

Mangia, Mangia . . . in 30! Menu

Effortless Chicken Parmesan and
Angel Hair Pasta with Easy Tomato Sauce

Cheddar Garlic Biscuits

Salad with Simple Balsamic Vinaigrette

Tiramisu for Two

If I Had One Dish!

Jumpin' Jumpin' Jambalaya

Creamy Shrimp and Grits

Chicken Marsala

Junior's Shepherd's Pie with Pure Bliss Mashed Potatoes

*h*e called to let you know how much you have been on his mind, and was wondering if you wanted to have company. He will be leaving work in an hour and wondered if he could stop by for a few.

Normally, you wouldn't even entertain the idea of having company over this late in the week. Your apartment is a wreck and you had planned on eating a bowl of cereal and catching up on your shows on your DVR. Cooking was not on your agenda tonight, but this is the guy you're trying to impress, right? This is the perfect opportunity to kick into Get 'Em Girls' mode and make it happen in the clutch.

So you run home, with an hour to work with. You put the dirty dishes in the dishwasher, make your bed, and throw your scattered clothes in the closet. Kick the shoes under the bed and run to the kitchen to see what you can whip up. There's not much, but we're sure we can make something happen with what you have.

The recipes in this section are quick, easy, and delicious. Enjoy them and *hurry up!*

30 Minutes or Less Tips

althought cooking can be pretty time-consuming, it doesn't have to be. Just follow some of our suggestions on speeding up the process and you will have plate to table in no time flat.

Make Sure Your Kitchen Is Organized

Store pots near the stove and utensils near your work area.

Learn to Multitask

Read each recipe carefully and look for spaces where you can incorporate 2 or 3 steps. For instance, while you're preheating the oven, begin boiling the water for pasta dishes and thawing your meat in the microwave.

Prepare Your Vegetables and Fresh Herbs Ahead of Time

When you come in from the grocery store, wash and store all your veggies/herbs in resealable plastic bags, making sure to wrap fresh herbs with a damp paper towel.

Shortcuts Work in a Pinch

Use bagged salad greens, pre-made pasta sauces, frozen vegetables, grated cheeses, and seasoning blends. Often, they save you time without taking away from the flavor of your dishes.

Try to Preplan Your Meals

You can have your meats thawed, marinated, and ready to cook if you've preplanned your meal.

Effortless Chicken Parmesan and Angel Hair Pasta

1 box (16 ounces) angel hair pasta, uncooked

Olive oil, for frying

1½ pounds chicken breast tenders

¼ teaspoon salt

¼ teaspoon ground black pepper

1 cup all-purpose flour

2 large eggs, lightly beaten

2 cups Italian-style bread crumbs

1½ cups shredded Parmesan cheese

1½ teaspoons dried thyme

1 cup chopped fresh flat-leaf parsley

½ teaspoon red pepper flakes

1½ cups Easy Tomato Sauce (following page)

½ cup shredded mozzarella cheese

*Q*uick and easy to make, but you can let him think you've been sweating in the kitchen all evening.

1 Preheat the oven to 350°F. Bring a large pot of lightly salted water to a boil over high heat.

2 Heat ½ inch olive oil in a large skillet over medium to medium-high heat. Season the chicken tenders with salt and pepper. Place flour in a shallow dish. Beat eggs in a second dish.

3 In a third dish, combine the bread crumbs, 1 cup of the Parmesan, the thyme, parsley, and red pepper flakes. Coat chicken in flour, then egg, then bread crumb mixture. In batches, cook chicken until deeply golden on each side, 4 to 5 minutes, and transfer to an 8 x 8-inch baking dish.

4 Pour a little of the Easy Tomato sauce on the chicken tenders and bake for 10 minutes or until cooked through.

5 Meanwhile, add the pasta and prepare according to package directions for al dente. Drain.

6 Remove the chicken from the oven and top with the mozzarella and the remaining ½ cup of Parmesan. Place back in the oven to melt the cheese, and remove. Coat the hot, cooked pasta lightly with sauce, top with the chicken, and serve.

Makes 4 to 6 servings

Easy Tomato Sauce

1 Place the olive oil, onions, green peppers (if using), and garlic in a large saucepan and cook over medium-low heat, stirring occasionally, for 10 minutes. **2** Add the tomatoes and tomato sauce and bring to a light boil. **3** Add the oregano, thyme, Italian seasoning, sugar (if using), and salt and pepper to your taste. Reduce the heat and simmer for 15 minutes. **4** Use immediately, or cool completely and store in an airtight jar. Sauce will keep for up to 3 days.

Makes about 4 cups

2 tablespoons extra virgin olive oil

1 small onion, chopped

1 small green bell pepper, seeded and chopped (optional)

2 cloves garlic, minced

2 cups canned crushed tomatoes, undrained

One 29-ounce can or two 15-ounce cans tomato sauce

1 teaspoon dried oregano

1 teaspoon dried thyme

½ teaspoon Italian seasoning blend

1 tablespoon sugar (optional)

Salt and ground black pepper

Cheddar Garlic Biscuits

2 cups baking mix (recommended: Bisquick)

⅔ cup milk

½ cup shredded Cheddar cheese

8 tablespoons unsalted butter, melted

¼ teaspoon garlic powder

*t*he garlic butter makes them so tasty! Be sure to refrigerate the leftovers (if there are any).

1 Preheat oven to 450°F.

2 Combine the baking mix, milk, and cheese in a medium bowl until a soft dough forms. Drop by the tablespoonful onto an ungreased cookie sheet.

3 Bake until golden brown, 8 to 10 minutes.

4 Mix the butter and garlic powder in a small bowl. Brush over the hot biscuits. Serve immediately.

Makes 6 to 8 servings

Salad with
Simple Balsamic Vinaigrette

1 In a jar with a tight-fitting lid, combine the olive oil, balsamic vinegar, and sugar. Season to taste with salt and pepper. Shake well and set aside.

2 Wash the lettuce leaves and dry well. Tear leaves into 1- to 2-inch pieces; transfer to a large bowl.

3 Top lettuce with tomatoes, cucumber, onion, and carrot. Toss well and drizzle liberally with vinaigrette.

Makes 2 to 4 servings

Simple Balsamic Vinaigrette

¼ **cup extra virgin olive oil**

3 **tablespoons balsamic vinegar**

½ **teaspoon sugar**

Salt and ground black pepper

Salad

1 **romaine lettuce heart, separated into leaves**

6 **cherry tomatoes, halved**

½ **cucumber, medium size, peeled and diced**

¼ **cup diced red onion**

1 **small carrot, peeled and shredded**

Tiramisu for Two

1 cup mascarpone cheese, softened

½ cup heavy cream

¼ cup plus 2 tablespoons confectioners' sugar

2 tablespoons coffee-flavored liqueur (recommended: Kahlua)

18 ladyfingers sponge cakes

¼ cup coffee, chilled

¼ cup chocolate-covered English toffee bits (recommended: Heath)

a creamy and delicious Get 'Em Girls' twist on a classic Italian dessert.

1 In a medium bowl with an electric mixer on medium-high, beat the mascarpone cheese, ¼ cup of the heavy cream, ¼ cup of the confectioners' sugar, and the liqueur until thickened.

2 Arrange 3 ladyfingers onto each of two dessert plates. Brush each ladyfinger with about 1 teaspoon of the coffee. Spread ½ of the mascarpone mixture over the ladyfingers and sprinkle with 1 teaspoon of the crumbled toffee bits.

3 Layer with another 3 ladyfingers, brushing each with another teaspoon of the coffee. Spread the remaining mascarpone mixture over the ladyfingers and sprinkle with 1 teaspoon of the toffee bits. Top with the last 3 ladyfingers.

4 Beat the remaining ¼ cup cream and confectioners' sugar in a small bowl with an electric mixer on medium-high, until soft peaks form, about 1 minute. Spread evenly over the top of the ladyfingers and sprinkle with the remaining toffee bits. Refrigerate for at least 1 hour to set and blend flavors.

Makes 2 servings

Jumpin' Jumpin' Jambalaya

*t*his recipe is a quick and easy way to add a little spice to an already spicy evening. Just because you're short on time, doesn't mean your food should be short on taste. Enjoy with steaming white rice and set the evening off, N'Awlins style.

1 Heat the olive oil in a Dutch oven over medium-high heat. Add the sausage, onion, bell pepper, celery, and garlic; cook and stir until onion becomes translucent, about 5 minutes. Stir in the shrimp; cook and stir until shrimp turn pink.

2 Stir in the tomato sauce, Cajun seasoning, salt, black pepper, and cayenne (if using) and cook until heated through. Serve immediately over rice and garnish with parsley and scallions.

Makes 6 to 8 servings

3 tablespoons olive oil

8 ounces andouille sausage, sliced thick

1 large onion, chopped

1 medium green pepper, seeded and chopped

3 stalks celery, chopped

2 cloves garlic, chopped

1½ pounds shrimp, peeled and deveined

Two 8-ounce cans tomato sauce

1½ teaspoons Cajun seasoning

1 teaspoon salt, plus more to taste

¼ teaspoon ground black pepper

¼ teaspoon cayenne pepper (optional)

Steamed white rice, for serving

Chopped fresh flat-leaf parsley, for garnish

2 scallions, chopped, for garnish

Creamy Shrimp and Grits

Grits

2 cups water

1¼ cups half-and-half

1 teaspoon salt

1 cup quick-cooking (not instant) grits

3 tablespoons unsalted butter

¼ teaspoon ground black pepper

Shrimp

1½ pounds large shrimp, peeled and deveined, tails on

Juice from ½ lemon

Kosher salt and ground black pepper

6 slices bacon

3 tablespoons finely chopped onion

2 tablespoons finely chopped green bell pepper

1 clove garlic, minced

2 tablespoons all-purpose flour

1 cup seafood or chicken stock

1 tablespoon finely chopped fresh flat-leaf parsley

1 tablespoon chopped scallion greens

*t*his dish reminds of days spent having brunch with my family in Charleston, South Carolina. It's a classic dish that is just as fast as it is delicious! —*Joan*

1 In a small pot, bring water, half-and-half, and salt to a boil. Slowly stir in the grits. Stir continuously until grits are mixed well. Let the pot return to a boil, cover with a tight-fitting lid and reduce the temperature to low.

2 Simmer for 20 to 30 minutes, stirring occasionally; add more water if necessary. Once grits have a smooth and creamy consistency, remove from heat. Stir in the butter and season with black pepper and additional salt, if necessary. Keep warm.

3 While the grits are cooking, toss the shrimp with lemon juice and season with salt and pepper; set aside.

4 Cook the bacon in a large skillet over medium-low heat until brown, but not crisp. Remove from the skillet and drain on a paper towel–lined platter; once cool enough to handle, coarsely chop and set aside.

5 Discard all but ¼ cup of the bacon fat from the skillet. Add the onions and green peppers. Cook and stir for 1 minute. Add the garlic. Continue to cook, stirring often, until the onions are translucent, about 3 minutes.

6 Sprinkle the flour over the onion mixture and stir with a wooden spoon to form a thick paste. Slowly pour in the stock, stirring continuously to avoid lumps and bring to a simmer. Reduce heat to low and stir in the shrimp and chopped bacon. Cook until the shrimp are pink, about 3 minutes. Season to taste with salt and pepper. Remove from heat and stir in the parsley and scallions.

7 To serve, spoon the hot grits onto individual serving plates and top with the shrimp mixture.

Makes 4 servings

Chicken Marsala

*O*ur twist on a classic that is great as an elegant meal for two or a quick meal just for yourself.

1 Place each chicken breast in between two pieces of parchment paper and pound with a kitchen mallet to ¼-inch thickness; set aside.

2 Combine the flour, salt, pepper, and oregano in a shallow bowl.

3 Heat the olive oil and 4 tablespoons of the butter together in a large skillet over medium heat. Coat the chicken in the seasoned flour, shaking off any excess flour and carefully place the chicken in the skillet. Cook, flipping once, until lightly browned on both sides, about 2 minutes per side. Transfer to a plate.

4 Add the mushrooms to the pan and cook, stirring frequently, until the mushrooms begin to brown. Turn the heat off and add the Marsala wine. Turn the heat back on to medium and bring the wine to a boil, scraping the bottom of the pan with a wooden spoon to remove any browned bits. When the wine has boiled down by half, add the chicken stock. Continue cooking until the sauce has thickened slightly, about 4 minutes.

5 Lower the heat to medium-low and return the chicken to the pan. Continue to cook until the chicken is cooked throughout and the sauce has thickened, 7 to 8 minutes. Stir in the remaining 2 tablespoons of butter and season to taste with additional salt and pepper. Serve immediately over rice or your favorite pasta.

Makes 4 servings

4 boneless and skinless chicken breast halves

½ cup all-purpose flour

1 teaspoon kosher salt

½ teaspoon ground black pepper

1 teaspoon dried oregano

¼ cup olive oil

6 tablespoons unsalted butter

1 cup sliced button mushrooms

½ cup Marsala wine

¼ cup chicken broth

Cooked rice or pasta, for serving

Junior's Shepherd's Pie

1 tablespoon vegetable oil

1½ pounds ground beef

1 teaspoon Get 'Em Girls' Essential Seasoning (page 29), plus more to taste

½ teaspoon ground black pepper, plus more to taste

1 small onion, finely chopped

2 tablespoons unsalted butter

2 tablespoons all-purpose flour

1 cup beef broth

Pure Bliss Mashed Potatoes (recipe follows)

½ cup frozen peas, thawed

1 cup shredded Cheddar cheese

½ teaspoon paprika

*t*his recipe was a staple in my house while growing up. My daddy used to put his foot in it—well, I put two! This is my daddy's recipe, kicked up! —*Jeniece*

1 Preheat the oven to 400°F.

2 Heat a large skillet over medium-high heat. Add the vegetable oil and the ground beef. Season meat with the Seasoning and black pepper. Brown and crumble meat with a fork until fully cooked and no longer pink. Stir in the onions and cook until the onions are translucent, about 5 minutes. Using a slotted spoon, transfer the beef to a bowl.

3 In a medium skillet, cook the butter and flour together over medium heat for 2 to 3 minutes. Gradually whisk in the broth. Bring the gravy up to a boil and then remove from heat. Season to taste with Seasoning and black pepper.

4 Begin layering an 8 x 8-inch baking dish with 1 cup of mashed potatoes, all of the meat, and the peas. Spoon the gravy over the top of the casserole and top with Cheddar cheese. Top with the remaining potatoes, making sure to spread evenly, and sprinkle with paprika.

5 Bake in the oven until potatoes are evenly browned, about 7 minutes. Let stand for 5 minutes and serve.

Makes 4 to 6 servings

---

8 medium unpeeled Red Bliss potatoes, washed and scrubbed

½ cup warm milk

6 tablespoons butter, softened

¼ cup sour cream

Salt and pepper

Pure Bliss Mashed Potatoes

1 Bring a large pot of lightly salted water to a boil over high heat. 2 Slice the potatoes ¼ inch thick and cook in the boiling water until fork tender, about 15 minutes. Drain and transfer to a large bowl. 3 Using a potato masher, mash potatoes until slightly smooth; a few lumps are fine. 4 Add the milk, butter, and sour cream to the potatoes. Mash until combined. Season with salt and pepper. Serve hot.

Makes 4 to 6 servings

Super Bowl Sundays

Sweet and Spicy Ribs

Cookie's Party Wings

Pizza Bites

Vegetable Tempura with Soy Dipping Sauce

Garlic and Basil Shrimp Skewers

Hot-Like-Fire Buffalo Wings

Sausage Rolls with Honey-Mustard Sauce

Crab Cakes

Joan's Hunch Punch

*h*is boys are on their way over to watch the game.

Do you:

A. Go in the bedroom and stay secluded until they leave?

B. Interrupt the game every five minutes to ask, "Is it over yet?"

C. Whip up some of your smoking buffalo wings with blue cheese dip, grab a cold Corona (with a slice of lime, of course), and grab a seat?

If you are a Get 'Em Girl, we know you chose C.

There is absolutely nothing wrong with playing hostess to your man's friends. You get to see the type of guys he chooses to run with, all the while forming an alliance with them that may come in handy one day.

Get 'Em Girls' Cheat Sheet

*h*ere we go ladies! You've decided you would go to a football game with your man, or you might just be watching it on the tube with him and his friends at home. Football can be very exciting while the game is in progress and during time-outs. Where else can we go to see 22 fit men running up and down a 100-yard field, tackling each other and dancing in the end zone, and, oh, okay . . . let's calm down! Believe us ladies, this is not just a "man's sport;" football is lots of fun for everyone who understands it.

Let's start with the basics: The object of the game is just like all other games—to outscore your opponent! Players do this by advancing the football into their opponent's end zone for as many touchdowns as possible.

Make sure you get dibs on the most comfortable seat in the house because you are going to be in it for a while. Games are divided into four 15-minute quarters. There is time for a bathroom break after the second quarter; this is referred to as "halftime." Games will run well over 60 minutes, due to halftime, TV timeouts, referee calls, team timeouts, and overtime, so be prepared to spend at least two hours per game!

Unfortunately, ladies, there can only be a total of 22 succulent bodies on the field (11 players from each team) at one time. A football team is composed of an offense, a defense, and special teams. The offense is on the field when your guy's favorite team has possession of the ball. Offensive players consist of the quarterback, running backs, wide receivers, offensive linemen, and tight end. The large, muscular men playing against them are called the defensive players. Their purpose is to line up and stop the offense from scoring. Defensive players consist of the cornerback, safeties, linebackers, defensive ends, and defensive tackles. Special teams participate during kicking situations (punts, field goals, and kickoffs). Special team players consist of the holder, kick returner, snapper, place kicker, punter, punt returners, and gunners.

Before each game the captains of the two teams meet in the center of the field with the referees (those short men with white pants and black-and-white striped shirts) for a coin toss. Whoever wins the coin toss has the option of starting the game by kicking the ball to the other team or having the other team kick the ball to them. So basically, the game begins with a *kickoff!* When one of the teams kicks off, the receiving team must catch the ball and proceed to advance as far as possible toward the kicking team's end zone.

Pandemonium in the stands, players dancing in the end zone, or fireworks on the field can only mean one thing . . . *touchdown!* Touchdowns are worth 6 points and are awarded when a player carries the ball or catches a pass in the opponent's end zone.

Sweet and Spicy Ribs

*a*dd a little spice to game night with these tender, succulent ribs.

1 Preheat oven to 350°F.

2 Heat the olive oil in a large Dutch oven over medium-high heat. Season ribs with salt and pepper and brown on all sides. Remove from heat and set aside.

3 In a food processor or blender, combine the honey, ketchup, ginger, and 1 to 2 chipotles with the adobo sauce. Blend until smooth. Taste and add more chipotles or honey, if desired. Pour half of the sauce over the ribs and toss.

4 Place the lid loosely on the Dutch oven, to allow the steam to escape and the sauce to thicken. Place the ribs in the oven.

5 Cook until the meat is very tender, 1½ to 2 hours. Remove from the oven and serve hot, with remaining sauce on the side.

Makes 4 to 6 servings

2 tablespoons plus 1½ teaspoons extra virgin olive oil

1 slab baby back ribs (about 3 pounds), skin removed and separated

Salt and ground black pepper

2 cups honey

2 cups ketchup

1½ teaspoons ground ginger

One 7-ounce can chipotles in adobo sauce

Cookie's Party Wings

Vegetable oil, for frying

1 pound chicken wings, disjointed and tips removed

1 tablespoon Get 'Em Girls' Essential Seasoning (page 29)

1½ teaspoons ground black pepper

1 teaspoon onion powder

1 teaspoon garlic powder

1 packet Sazón with cilantro and annatto

½ cup buttermilk

2 cups all-purpose flour

*W*ings! The perfect meal at any party. These wings are crispy and full of flavor. Add a little ranch or blue cheese dressing, or just a bit of hot sauce, and they are good to go.

1 Preheat oven to 350°F.

2 In a deep fryer or high-sided skillet, heat 3 inches of oil to 360°F.

3 Wash the chicken wings and pat dry. In a small bowl combine the Seasoning, black pepper, onion powder, garlic powder, and Sazón. In a separate bowl combine the buttermilk, 1½ teaspoons of the seasoning mixture, and ½ cup of the flour. Mix well to make a batter.

4 Season the chicken with 2 teaspoons of the seasoning mixture. In a large bowl, combine the remaining flour with the remaining seasoning mixture. Dip the wings one at a time into the batter, allowing excess to drip off, and toss with the flour to coat completely.

5 Working in batches, carefully add the chicken to the deep fryer and cook for 6 to 8 minutes, moving and turning frequently with tongs.

6 Remove the chicken with a slotted spoon and drain on a paper towel–lined platter.

7 Transfer the chicken to a cookie sheet and bake until crisp, about 10 minutes.

Makes 6 to 8 servings

Pizza Bites

*W*ho needs delivery when you've got a Get 'Em Girl? These little bite-size pizzas are so good, your man's friends might start placing orders.

1 Preheat the oven to 450°F.

2 Using a 3½-inch round biscuit cutter, cut rounds from pizza shell to make 10 individual crusts. Place the pizza rounds on a cookie sheet, top with sauce, and cover with mozzarella. Sprinkle with Parmesan and top with your favorite topping.

3 Bake until the cheese is melted, approximately 10 minutes. Serve hot.

Makes 10 pieces

2 large storebought prebaked pizza shells (recommended: Boboli)

2 cups Easy Tomato Sauce (page 115)

1 cup shredded mozzarella cheese

¼ cup freshly grated Parmesan cheese

Toppings of your choice, such as pepperoni slices, crumbled cooked Italian sausage, or sliced grilled chicken

Vegetable Tempura with Soy Dipping Sauce

2 cups all-purpose flour

½ teaspoon salt

2 cups chilled seltzer

Vegetable oil, for frying

2 pounds assorted raw vegetables, washed and patted dry:

Zucchini, sliced into ½-inch-thick sticks

Broccoli florets

Carrots, cut into ½-inch-thick slices

Cauliflower florets

*f*or the veggie lovers, these are bite-size and delicious. Serve with the delectable Soy Dipping Sauce alongside for added flavor.

1 In a large bowl, whisk together the flour and salt. Slowly add 1 cup seltzer, whisking mixture until smooth. Let the batter stand for 10 minutes. If necessary, thin batter with remaining seltzer, pouring in ¼ cup at a time until you reach the consistency of thin pancake batter.

2 In a deep-fryer or high-sided skillet, heat 3 inches of vegetable oil to 375°F. Working in batches, dip the vegetables in the batter, letting excess drip off. Carefully add vegetables to the deep fryer.

3 Fry until golden brown. Remove the vegetables with a slotted spoon and drain on a paper towel–lined platter. Serve immediately.

Makes 6 to 8 servings

2 scallions, white and green parts, sliced

2 tablespoons rice wine vinegar

½ cup soy sauce

1 tablespoon grated fresh ginger

Soy Dipping Sauce

Combine all ingredients in a medium bowl and stir to mix well. Serve alongside the Vegetable Tempura.

Makes about ½ cup

Garlic and Basil Shrimp Skewers

*t*hese tasty skewers will have your guests interested in more than just the game!

1 In a wide shallow glass bowl, combine olive oil and melted butter. Stir in the lemon juice, mustard, basil, garlic, salt, and pepper. Add shrimp and toss to coat. Cover and refrigerate for 1 hour.

2 Preheat a lightly oiled grill pan over medium-high heat. Remove shrimp from marinade and thread onto bamboo skewers. Arrange skewers on the grill pan. Cook 4 to 6 minutes, turning once, until pink.

Makes 9 skewers

TAKE NOTE

Soak bamboo skewers for 15 to 20 minutes in warm water to avoid flame-ups and splintering.

2 tablespoons olive oil

4 tablespoons unsalted butter, melted

Juice of 1 lemon

2½ tablespoons brown prepared mustard

¼ cup minced fresh basil

3 cloves garlic, minced

½ teaspoon kosher salt

½ teaspoon ground white pepper

3 pounds extra large shrimp, peeled and deveined

Hot-Like-Fire Buffalo Wings

2½ pounds chicken wings, disjointed, with tips removed

½ cup hot pepper sauce

5 tablespoons butter, melted

*t*he ultimate game day food. These are hot, tangy, and damn good! Enjoy them with our blue cheese dressing (see page 107) and a cold beer to get the party started right.

1 Preheat the oven to 425°F.

2 Wash the chicken wings and pat dry. Spread the wings in a shallow roasting pan and bake wings for 1 hour. Remove from the oven.

3 In a large bowl, combine the hot pepper sauce and melted butter. Toss in chicken wings and mix to coat thoroughly. Let sit for 5 minutes and serve.

Makes 6 to 8 servings

Sausage Rolls with Honey-Mustard Sauce

*t*his is a grown folks' version of "pigs-in-a-blanket." Nothing like having a house full of grown men and only cocktail franks to feed 'em—you are bound to have a problem! Add the spicy and sweet Honey-Mustard Sauce for good dipping.

1 Preheat oven to 350°F.

2 Unroll crescent rolls and separate into 6 pieces. Roll each piece of kielbasa in a crescent roll and place on a cookie sheet. Gently brush beaten egg over the dough.

3 Bake until the crescent rolls are golden brown and puffed, 15 to 20 minutes. Serve with Honey-Mustard Sauce.

Makes 6 servings

One 8-ounce can refrigerated crescent rolls

One 16-ounce package Polska kielbasa, cut into 6 equal pieces

1 large egg, beaten

Honey-Mustard Sauce

In a small bowl, combine all ingredients and stir to mix well. Transfer to a serving bowl and serve alongside the sausage rolls.

Makes 2¼ cups

1½ cups mayonnaise

¼ cup Dijon mustard

½ cup honey

Crab Cakes

Crab Cakes

1 tablespoon olive oil

2 scallions, finely chopped (white and green parts)

½ pound jumbo lump crabmeat

⅓ cup crushed crackers (recommended: Ritz)

1 large egg, slightly beaten

1 tablespoon mayonnaise

1 teaspoon dry mustard

½ teaspoon garlic powder

¼ teaspoon crab boil seasoning (recommended: Old Bay)

1 teaspoon salt

½ teaspoon ground black pepper

Dash of cayenne pepper

All-purpose flour, for dusting

½ cup vegetable oil

Classic Tartar Sauce

1 cup mayonnaise

1 tablespoon sweet pickle relish

1 tablespoon minced onion

Salt and ground black pepper, to taste

Mango Mayo

½ cup mayonnaise

3 tablespoons mango nectar

1 teaspoon fresh lime juice

Salt and ground black pepper, to taste

*b*ring the harbor to your home with these delicious lump crab cakes. Serve with classic Tartar Sauce or delicious Mango Mayo.

Crab Cakes

1 Heat the olive oil in a medium skillet over medium-high heat. Add the scallions; cook and stir until tender. Remove from the heat and allow to cool.

2 Meanwhile, in a large bowl, mix together the crabmeat, crackers, egg, mayonnaise, dry mustard, garlic powder, crab boil seasoning, salt, black pepper, and cayenne pepper. Shape into ½-inch-thick patties and dust with flour. Refrigerate the crab cakes on a parchment paper–lined platter for 1 hour, to allow cakes to set.

3 Heat the vegetable oil in a large skillet over medium heat. In batches, carefully place crab cakes in the pan and fry until golden brown on each side, 8 to 10 minutes. Drain briefly on a paper towel–lined platter. Serve warm with Tartar Sauce or Mango Mayo.

Classic Tartar Sauce

4 In a small bowl, combine all ingredients and stir to mix well. Refrigerate until ready to serve.

Mango Mayo

5 In a small bowl, combine all ingredients and stir to mix well. Refrigerate until ready to serve.

Makes 4 servings

Joan's Hunch Punch

*m*y version of a Carolina classic punch; it's a staple at tail-gate parties and family reunions. Sip slowly and stay away from the Spades table!

1 In a 5-gallon container mix the Hawaiian Punch and pineapple juice. Stir in the peach liqueur, rum, and vodka. Refrigerate for 6 hours, preferably overnight.

2 Before serving stir in frozen pineapple chunks and peach slices.

Makes 15 sixteen-ounce servings

One 2-liter bottle Hawaiian Punch

Two 46-ounce cans pineapple juice

One 750ml bottle peach liqueur (recommended: Dekuyper's Peach Schnapps)

Two 750ml bottles light rum (recommended: Bacardi)

One 375ml bottle vodka

4 cups frozen chunks pineapple

4 cups frozen sliced peaches

Hot Plate Love

Dorm Room Passion Menu
Hearty Black Bean Chili with Homemade Tortilla Chips
Chicken and Broccoli Stir-Fry
Baked Spaghetti
Aunt Nae's Burritos
Cherry Granita

Entry-Level Loving Menu
Shrimp Scampi with Linguini and Toasty Garlic Bread
Tantalizingly Tangy Meatloaf with Mama Cookie's BBQ Sauce
Rigatoni Bolognese
Stuffed Pork Chops
Comforting Chicken Pot Pie
Loaded Sweet Potatoes
Fudge Brownie Bowl

In college, I dated a special guy and I always wanted to cook for him, however, I did not have the money to make anything happen. Although I was famous for my cinnamon rolls and Kool-Aid—thank God for meal plans.

Shakara *New York, NY*

*h*ot Plate Love is dedicated to anybody on a *serious* budget. Whether you are a struggling college student, a struggling graduate (with student loans kicking in), or if the check didn't quite cut it this week . . . this one is for you!

Plan meals: By planning your meals ahead you can make the best use of leftovers. If Monday is spaghetti with meat sauce, that same meat sauce can be transformed into a wonderfully hearty chili on Tuesday—just by adding a few simple ingredients. Freeze any of the meat sauce/chili that you don't eat in individual freezer bags for quick meals later on.

Shop smart: Before you even think about going to the supermarket, create a shopping list, making sure to check your cabinets and refrigerator for ingredients you have on hand. Next, tuck your cute little tail between your legs and get out the scissors and Sunday paper—clip those coupons, but only for things you need! One other thing: grab a sandwich or protein bar to eat before hitting the supermarket. There's nothing more expensive than going food shopping on an empty stomach.

Don't be afraid to buy store-brand foods: Okay, there are no cool green mascots and the labels look really, really generic; but so what if the taste is the same, who cares? Canned corn is canned corn—but don't fool yourself into thinking Fruity Oh's and Fruit Loops are one and the same. Save where you can, but splurge a little where you need to.

Hearty Black Bean Chili with Homemade Tortilla Chips

*t*his delicious and filling one-pot dish can be stretched further than you might imagine. Trust us—we live in New York City, remember? So even if you invite that cute Kappa you met at the library last week over for dinner, there will still be enough to last you a day or two . . . or three.

1 Heat the olive oil in a large stock pot over medium heat. Add the onions and green peppers to the pot; cook and stir until the onions are translucent, about 5 minutes. Add the ground turkey to the pot and cook, stirring, until no pink shows.

2 Stir in the beans, tomatoes, tomato sauce, chili powder, cumin, garlic powder, salt, black pepper, and cayenne, and reduce the heat to low. Cover and simmer until the flavors are well blended, 1½ to 2 hours.

3 Serve hot over white rice or with Homemade Tortilla Chips.

Makes 6 servings

1 tablespoon olive oil

1 small onion, diced

1 small green pepper, seeded and diced

2 pounds ground turkey breast

One 15-ounce can black beans, undrained

One 14.5-ounce can crushed tomatoes

One 8-ounce can tomato sauce

¼ cup chili powder

1 teaspoon ground cumin

1 teaspoon garlic powder

1 teaspoon salt

½ teaspoon ground black pepper

⅛ teaspoon cayenne pepper

Homemade Tortilla Chips

1 Heat the vegetable oil in a large skillet over medium heat. Meanwhile, quarter the tortillas and separate. **2** Carefully add the tortillas wedges to the hot oil. Fry 1 to 2 minutes per side and remove. Drain on a paper towel-lined platter. Season to taste with salt while still hot. Serve warm with chili or your favorite salsa.

Makes 2 to 4 servings

¼ cup vegetable oil

6 small flour tortillas

Salt

Salsa, for serving (optional)

Chicken and Broccoli Stir-Fry

Two 3-ounce packages ramen noodles

One 8-ounce package cooked chicken breast (recommended: Perdue Shortcuts)

3 tablespoons margarine

1 small onion, cut into 1-inch strips

1 small red bell pepper, cut into 1-inch strips

1½ cups frozen broccoli florets, thawed

Salt and ground black pepper

½ teaspoon garlic powder

1 tablespoon all-purpose flour

¼ cup water

1 tablespoon low-sodium soy sauce

*C*heap eats at their best!

1 To prepare the ramen noodles, bring a large pot of water to a boil. Discard ramen soup base. Add noodles and cook for 3 minutes. Drain and set aside.

2 Cut chicken breast in ½-inch pieces. In a large skillet, melt the margarine over medium heat. Add the chicken, onion, and bell pepper. Cook and stir until onions are translucent.

3 Add the broccoli and season to taste with salt and black pepper and the garlic powder. Continue to cook for another 5 minutes, stirring occasionally.

4 In a small bowl, mix the flour and water until dissolved. Add the flour mixture and soy sauce to the skillet. Stir occasionally and let thicken, about 2 minutes.

5 Remove from heat and add the prepared ramen noodles, tossing to coat the noodles. Adjust seasoning with salt and pepper as necessary, and serve immediately.

Makes 4 servings

Baked Spaghetti

*t*oday is the day for you to embrace your fears. You've walked by your dorm kitchen countless times. The cafeteria has become a bore and you just can't make it home to Grandma's. Grab your boo or suitemates and enjoy this scrumptious pasta dish.

1 Preheat the oven to 350°F. Bring a large pot of salted water to a boil over high heat. Add the spaghetti and prepare according to package directions for al dente. Drain.

2 In a Dutch oven, heat the olive oil over medium-high heat. Add the ground beef, breaking the beef up well with a wooden spoon until fully cooked and no pink remains. Using a skimmer or large spoon, remove the fat from the meat. Add the spaghetti sauce, onions, green bell pepper, garlic, Seasoning, black pepper, parsley, oregano, thyme, and sugar. Bring to a boil over high heat, then reduce heat and simmer for 10 minutes.

3 Cover the bottom of an 8 x 8-inch baking dish with sauce. Add a layer of pasta and then a little less than half of each cheese. Repeat layers, ending with sauce.

4 Bake for 20 minutes.

5 Top the casserole with the remaining cheese, return it to the oven, and bake until the cheese is melted and bubbly, about 5 minutes more. Remove from the oven and allow to rest for 5 minutes before serving.

Makes 4 to 6 servings

8 ounces uncooked thin spaghetti

2 tablespoons extra virgin olive oil

1½ pounds ground beef

One 26-ounce jar traditional-style spaghetti sauce

1 small onion, chopped

1 medium green bell pepper, seeded and chopped

2 cloves garlic, chopped

1½ teaspoons Get 'Em Girls' Essential Seasoning (page 29)

½ teaspoon ground black pepper

½ cup chopped fresh flat-leaf parsley

½ teaspoon dried oregano

½ teaspoon dried thyme

1 teaspoon sugar

1 cup shredded sharp Cheddar cheese

1 cup shredded mozzarella cheese

¼ cup freshly grated Parmesan cheese

Aunt Nae's Burritos

1 pound ground beef

1 pound bulk breakfast sausage
(recommended: Jimmy Dean)

One 16-ounce can refried beans

One 1.5- to 1.62-ounce package
burrito seasoning

¼ teaspoon granulated garlic or
garlic powder

½ teaspoon chili powder

4 burrito-size tortillas

1 cup grated Cheddar cheese

1 cup shredded mozzarella cheese

1 cup sour cream

One 12-ounce jar jalapeños, sliced
(optional), for garnish

1 jar picante sauce (optional)

i could always count on my aunt Renee to send me back to UNC with a couple of her tasty burritos (without the jalapeños—of course!) —*Shakara*

1 In a large skillet over medium-high heat, cook the beef, stirring occasionally, until no pink remains. Using a slotted spoon, transfer the beef to a large bowl. Drain any remaining fat.

2 Add the sausage to the skillet. Cook, stirring, until the sausage is browned and no pink remains.

3 Add the beef back to the skillet and add the beans, burrito seasoning, garlic, and chili powder. Cover and reduce heat to low; cook until the mixture begins to thicken, 10 to 15 minutes.

4 Place the tortillas on a flat surface and fill with the meat mixture. Top with ¼ cup of each cheese and a dollop of sour cream. To roll the burrito: gently fold the top of the tortilla toward you while folding the ends into the center. Serve with jalapeños and picante sauce, if desired.

Makes 4 servings

Cherry Granita

*O*kay, it's just frozen Kool-Aid—but doesn't it sound good?

1 In a large pitcher, combine the water and drink mix, stirring until mix is completely dissolved. Pour into an 8 x 8-inch baking dish.

2 Freeze until firm, about 3 hours, removing dish from the freezer every 30 minutes to scrape with a metal spoon, leaving scrapings in the dish to harden.

3 Remove from freezer 10 minutes before serving to soften. Scoop into bowls, garnish each with a maraschino cherry, and serve immediately.

Makes 10 servings

4 cups cold water

⅓ cup cherry-flavored presweetened drink mix (recommended: Kool-Aid)

Maraschino cherries, for garnish

Shrimp Scampi with Linguini and Toasty Garlic Bread

One 16-ounce package linguini

5 tablespoons extra virgin olive oil, plus more for drizzling

5 tablespoons unsalted butter

2 shallots, finely diced

2 cloves garlic, minced

1 pound shrimp, peeled and deveined

1 teaspoon kosher salt

¼ teaspoon ground black pepper

¼ cup dry white wine

1 teaspoon lemon juice

¼ cup finely chopped fresh flat-leaf parsley

*Y*ou've got your first check and your first love—splurge a little!

1 Bring a large pot of lightly salted water to a boil. Cook pasta according to package instructions for al dente. Drain and set aside.

2 Meanwhile, heat 3 tablespoons of the olive oil and 3 tablespoons of the butter in a large skillet over medium-high heat. Add the shallots and garlic to the pan; cook and stir until the shallots are translucent, 2 to 3 minutes.

3 Season the shrimp with salt and pepper and add to the pan. Cook until they turn pink, 2 to 3 minutes. Remove the shrimp from the pan and set aside.

4 Add the wine and lemon juice to the pan and bring to a boil. Add the remaining 2 tablespoons of butter and 2 tablespoons of olive oil. When the butter has melted, return the shrimp to the pan.

5 Remove from heat and add the parsley and cooked pasta. Toss to coat the pasta and drizzle with a bit more olive oil. Serve immediately, with Toasty Garlic Bread.

Makes 4 servings

---

1 loaf Italian bread

8 tablespoons butter

3 cloves garlic, minced

Toasty Garlic Bread

1 Preheat the broiler. **2** Cut the Italian bread in half lengthwise. Place butter and garlic in a large roasting pan and heat on the top of the stove until the butter melts. **3** Place the bread halves cut side up on a cookie sheet and toast under the broiler until golden brown. Remove from the broiler and place in melted butter mixture, cut side down. Move the bread around in the butter mixture to saturate the bread. **4** Remove bread, slice, and serve hot.

Makes 4 servings

Tantalizingly Tangy Meatloaf with Mama Cookie's BBQ Sauce

a spicy twist on an ordinary meatloaf.

1 Preheat the oven to 350°F.

2 Using your hands, mix together the ground beef, bread crumbs, onion, egg, seasoning, black pepper, and tomato sauce in a large bowl.

3 Form the mixture into a loaf and place in a shallow baking pan. Pour 1½ cups BBQ sauce over the meatloaf

4 Bake for 1½ hours, basting every 15 minutes with the pan juices, until a meat thermometer reads 160°F when inserted in the center of the meatloaf. Remove from oven and let sit for 5 minutes before slicing.

Makes 6 servings

1½ pounds ground beef

1 cup plain dried bread crumbs

1 small onion, diced fine

1 large egg, lightly beaten

1½ teaspoons Get 'Em Girls' Essential Seasoning (page 29)

½ teaspoon ground black pepper

½ cup tomato sauce

1½ cups Mama Cookie's BBQ Sauce

Mama Cookie's BBQ Sauce

1 In a medium saucepan over medium heat, stir together the tomato sauce, brown sugar, vinegar, mustard, Worcestershire sauce, and onion and garlic powders. Bring to a boil. Cook for 1 minute, stirring constantly to avoid scorching. **2** Reduce the heat to low. Cook and stir for about 15 minutes. Remove from heat and use immediately or let sauce cool completely and bottle in an airtight jar, to keep for up to 1 week.

Makes about 2 cups

1½ cups tomato sauce

3 tablespoons light brown sugar

3 tablespoons distilled white vinegar

2 tablespoons Dijon mustard

2 tablespoons Worcestershire sauce

¼ teaspoon onion powder

¼ teaspoon garlic powder

Rigatoni Bolognese

¼ cup extra virgin olive oil

1 small onion, chopped

⅓ cup peeled, chopped carrot

¼ cup chopped celery

2 cloves garlic, minced

1 pound ground beef

Salt and ground black pepper

½ cup dry white wine

1 cup chicken broth

One 28-ounce can whole tomatoes, hand crushed, with their juice

One 8-ounce can tomato sauce

½ teaspoon dried oregano

2 fresh basil leaves

One 16-ounce box rigatoni

½ cup freshly grated Parmesan cheese

1 In a large Dutch oven, heat the olive oil over medium heat. Add the onion, carrot, and celery and cook, stirring often, until the vegetables are tender but not brown, about 7 minutes. Stir in the garlic and cook, stirring often, until the garlic is fragrant, about 1 minute. Add the beef and season with 1 teaspoon salt and ½ teaspoon black pepper. Cook, breaking up the meat with the back of a wooden spoon, just until the meat is no longer pink, about 8 minutes.

2 Add the wine to the meat mixture and cook, stirring frequently, for 10 minutes. Stir in the chicken stock, tomatoes with their juice, and tomato sauce. Add the oregano and basil. Bring to a boil, then reduce the heat to low and simmer until the sauce is thick, 1 to 1½ hours. Remove from heat and season to taste with additional salt and black pepper.

3 Meanwhile, bring a large pot of salted water to a boil. Add the rigatoni. Cook according to the package directions until just tender. Drain and toss the pasta with ½ of the meat sauce. Serve topped with additional meat sauce and Parmesan cheese.

Make 4 to 6 servings

Stuffed Pork Chops

1 Preheat the oven to 350°F. Lightly butter a shallow baking dish and set aside. Cut a horizontal pocket into each pork chop to the bone. Season with salt and pepper, making sure to season inside the pork chop as well. Place the bread cubes in a medium bowl and set aside.

2 Cook the sausage in a large skillet over medium heat until it begins to brown. Drain off fat. Add the onion, celery, and mushrooms and cook, stirring often, until the onions are translucent, about 10 minutes.

3 Mix the sausage mixture into the bread cubes. Add the chicken stock, melted butter, and poultry seasoning, and additional salt and black pepper. Mix until thoroughly combined.

4 Place the pork chops in the prepared baking dish and lightly stuff the pork chops with the stuffing mixture, placing any remaining stuffing mixture around the pork chops. Bake uncovered for 1 hour; cover with aluminum foil and continue baking until pork chops are done, about 15 minutes.

Makes 4 servings

4 bone-in pork chops, 1¼ to 1½ inches thick

Salt and ground black pepper

½ cup white bread cubes, lightly toasted

½ pound bulk sage sausage (recommended: Jimmy Dean)

2 tablespoons chopped onion

2 tablespoons chopped celery

4 ounces button mushrooms, sliced

3 tablespoons chicken stock

2 tablespoons unsalted butter, melted

¼ teaspoon poultry seasoning

Comforting Chicken Pot Pie

1 sheet frozen puff pastry

2 tablespoons vegetable oil

1½ pounds skinless and boneless chicken thighs

Get 'Em Girls' Essential Seasoning (page 29)

Ground black pepper

¼ teaspoon granulated garlic or garlic powder

8 tablespoons unsalted butter

1½ cups diced Russet potatoes, medium size

¼ cup chopped onion

One 10-ounce package frozen mixed vegetables, thawed

½ cup all-purpose flour

1 cup chicken broth

1½ cups heavy cream

*d*elicious and soul-soothing, this pot pie is one to write home about. Just as delicious with storebought chicken; make it your own by adding different veggies and spices!

1 Preheat the oven to 350°F. Set the puff pastry out to thaw slightly.

2 Heat the vegetable oil in a large skillet over medium-high heat. Wash and pat dry the chicken and season with ¼ teaspoon Seasoning and ¼ teaspoon black pepper, and garlic powder. Add the chicken to the skillet; cook, stirring occasionally, until cooked through, 7 to 8 minutes. Remove the chicken from the pan and dice into ½-inch cubes and set aside.

3 In a large saucepan over medium heat, melt the butter. Add the potatoes and onion. Cook and stir until the onions are translucent, about 5 minutes. Add the mixed vegetables. Cook and stir for an additional 10 minutes. Gradually add the flour, stirring constantly.

4 Combine the chicken broth and heavy cream in a small bowl. Slowly stir into the vegetable mixture. Cook over medium heat, stirring constantly, until it reaches the consistency of thick gravy and coats the back of a spoon. Stir in ½ teaspoon Seasoning and ¼ teaspoon black pepper. Stir in the diced chicken and season with additional Seasoning and pepper.

5 Pour the chicken mixture into a 13 x 9-inch baking dish and top with the puff pastry and press firmly to adhere. Cut off any excess pastry on the sides and cut vents into the pastry dough.

6 Bake until the crust is a golden brown and the sauce begins to bubble on the sides, 35 to 40 minutes.

Makes 4 to 6 servings

Loaded Sweet Potatoes

1 Pierce the sweet potatoes all over with a fork. Place on a paper towel–lined microwave-safe plate, about 1 inch apart.

2 Cook on high power for 6 to 8 minutes, turning over halfway through.

3 Meanwhile, in a small bowl, combine the brown sugar and cinnamon and set aside.

4 Remove sweet potatoes from the microwave and let stand for 5 minutes. Split lengthwise and fluff the meat with a fork. Dot each half with 1 tablespoon of butter and sprinkle evenly with the brown sugar mixture. Serve immediately.

Makes 2 servings

2 medium unpeeled orange-flesh sweet potatoes, washed and scrubbed

2 tablespoons light brown sugar

½ teaspoon ground cinnamon

4 tablespoons unsalted butter, room temperature

Fudge Brownie Bowl

One 19.8-ounce package fudge brownie mix (recommended: Duncan Hines)

1 pint vanilla ice cream

Chocolate fudge ice cream topping

1 Prepare the fudge brownies according to the package directions for an 8 x 8-inch baking pan. Let cool completely.

2 While brownies are cooling, set ice cream out to soften. Pour the fudge topping into a microwave-safe dish and heat in microwave for 10 seconds on high power. Remove and set aside.

3 To assemble, cut brownies into 9 squares. Place two brownies in each dessert bowl and spoon the hot fudge on top of the brownie squares. Arrange a scoop of ice cream in the middle of the two brownies and serve immediately.

Makes 4 to 5 servings

Sweet Tooth

Meet-the-Parents Carrot Cake
Chocolate Toffee Trifle
Easy Bananas Foster
Oatmeal Cookie Cheesecake
Cocoa Cure Chocolate Cake
Easy Peach Cobbler
Creamy Caramel Cake
Put-It-On-Him Cake
Like-Sunshine Lemon Cake
Crumbly Caramel Apple Pie
Just Peachy Bread Pudding
Peachtini
Caramel Appletini

*i*f you want to end the perfect meal correctly, you have to have something sweet to send him off with. Whether it's sweet and sticky caramel cake, or warm apple pie and homemade ice cream (yes, we said homemade—don't be a slouch now) you know the meal isn't complete without something sweet. We are sure you'll find a recipe or two in this section that will have his sweet tooth screaming for more.

Meet-the-Parents Carrot Cake

*h*e invited you to his family's backyard barbecue—don't you dare go empty-handed! This cake will definitely leave a good impression with those closest to him.

1 Preheat oven to 325°F. Lightly butter and flour a 13 x 9-inch baking pan, tapping out the excess flour, and set aside.

2 Sift together into a large bowl the flour, baking soda, baking powder, salt, cinnamon, and allspice. Set aside. In another large bowl, using an electric mixer at high speed, beat the sugar, oil, eggs, and vanilla extract until well combined, about 1 minute.

3 With the mixer turned to low speed, beat in the flour mixture, scraping down the sides of the bowl as needed. Mix until smooth. Using a wooden spoon, stir in the carrots, pineapple, nuts, and flaked coconut (if using). Spread evenly in the prepared pan.

4 Bake until the top springs back when pressed lightly in the center, 35 to 40 minutes. Cool completely in the pan on a wire rack.

5 While the cake is cooling, in a medium bowl, beat the cream cheese, confectioners' sugar, and vanilla and almond extracts with an electric mixer on low speed until smooth. Fold in the whipped topping with a silicone spatula.

6 Once the cake is completely cooled, spread the frosting over the top of the cake. Cut into 10 to 12 pieces.

Makes 10 to 12 servings

Cake

2 cups all-purpose flour

1½ teaspoons baking soda

2 teaspoons baking powder

1 teaspoon salt

1½ teaspoons ground cinnamon

⅛ teaspoon ground allspice

2 cups granulated sugar

1½ cups vegetable oil

4 large eggs, room temperature

1 teaspoon vanilla extract

2¾ cups shredded carrots

One 8-ounce can crushed pineapple, drained

¾ cup chopped walnuts

½ cup sweetened flaked coconut (optional)

Frosting

One 8-ounce package cream cheese, room temperature

One 1-pound box confectioners' sugar

½ teaspoon vanilla extract

½ teaspoon almond extract

One 8-ounce container frozen whipped topping, thawed

Chocolate Toffee Trifle

Cake Mix

One 18.25-ounce package devil's food cake mix

1½ cups water

⅓ cup vegetable oil

3 large eggs

2 cups heavy cream

2 tablespoons confectioners' sugar

1 teaspoon vanilla

Six 1⅛-ounce chocolate-covered English toffee bars, frozen (recommended: Heath Bars)

*l*ooks good and tastes even better. This simple dessert is great for a get-together because it's easy to make and everyone can help themselves.

1 Prepare the cake according to package directions for a 13 x 9-inch cake. Let cool for 5 minutes in the pan, then transfer to a wire rack to cool completely. Once cool, cut into ½-inch cubes and set aside.

2 In a large, chilled bowl, whip the cream with an electric mixer until soft peaks form. Beat in sugar and vanilla until stiff peaks form. Do not overbeat, as cream will become lumpy and butterlike. Cover with plastic wrap and refrigerate until needed.

3 Place toffee bars in a resealable plastic bag and crush with a hammer.

4 In a large trifle dish or glass bowl, layer in this order:

one-third of the cake cubes
one-third of the whipped cream
one-third of the toffee

5 Repeat layers twice more and cover with plastic wrap. Refrigerate for at least 4 hours before serving.

Makes 6 servings

MAKE IT YOUR OWN

Drizzle ¼ cup of Kahlua liqueur onto the cake cubes prior to layering the trifle.

SHORTCUT

Save yourself some time! If you are in a rush, or just not in the mood to whip your own cream—substitute the whipped cream ingredients with two 8-ounce containers of frozen whipped topping.

Easy Bananas Foster

a classic New Orleans dessert of warm caramelized bananas and vanilla ice cream.

Melt the butter in a large saucepan over medium heat. Stir in the brown sugar, rum, vanilla, cinnamon, and salt. Lower the heat and cook just until mixture begins to bubble, about 2 minutes. Stir in the bananas and cook for 2 minutes. Remove from heat and serve over scoops of vanilla ice cream atop pound cake slices.

Makes 4 servings

4 tablespoons unsalted butter

1 cup dark brown sugar, tightly packed

¼ cup dark rum

2 teaspoons vanilla extract

1 teaspoon ground cinnamon

⅛ teaspoon salt

3 bananas, peeled and sliced

4 scoops vanilla ice cream

4 slices pound cake (storebought is okay)

Oatmeal Cookie Cheesecake

Cookie Crust

1½ cups quick-cooking oats (not instant or old-fashioned)

1 cup all-purpose flour

½ cup firmly packed light brown sugar

½ teaspoon ground cinnamon

¼ teaspoon salt

10 tablespoons unsalted butter, melted

Cheesecake

Four 8-ounce packages cream cheese, room temperature

1½ cups granulated sugar

¼ cup cornstarch

1 tablespoon vanilla extract

3 large eggs

¾ cup heavy cream

One 21-ounce can apple pie filling or 2½ cups of your favorite fruit compote

*t*here is a story behind this cheesecake—which we'll save for *The Get 'Em Girls' Guide to Dealing with the Salty Ex*! However, this cheesecake is banging! Enjoy it with a sweet Muscat dessert wine and brush your shoulder off.

1 Preheat the oven to 350°F. Generously butter a 9-inch springform pan and set aside.

2 In a large bowl, mix together the oats, flour, brown sugar, cinnamon, and salt. Add the melted butter to the oats mixture and mix well. Using your hand or the back of a large spoon, press the oat mixture evenly into the bottom and up the sides of the pan. Bake until golden brown, about 10 minutes. Set aside to cool while making filling. Leave oven at 350°F.

3 In a large bowl, using an electric mixer on low, beat together one package of the cream cheese, ½ cup of the sugar, and cornstarch. Beat until creamy, about 3 minutes. Beat in the remaining cream cheese.

4 Increase the mixer speed to high and beat in the remaining cup of sugar and the vanilla. Beat in the eggs, one at a time, scraping down the side of the bowl with a silicone spatula, as needed. Blend in the heavy cream. Mix just enough to combine the cream, being careful not to overmix the batter. Gently spoon the cheese filling on top of the oatmeal cookie crust. Bake cheesecake until the center barely jiggles when you shake the pan, about 1 hour.

5 Turn the oven off after 1 hour and open the oven door slightly. Let the cake cool in the oven for 1 hour. Once the cake has cooled, remove and cover with plastic wrap and refrigerate until it's completely cold, at least 4 hours or overnight.

6 Remove the sides of the springform pan. Slide the cake off the bottom of the pan onto a serving plate. Top with the apple pie filling or fruit compote of your choice.

Makes 12 servings

Cocoa Cure Chocolate Cake

*W*arning—chocolate overload! This is the chocolate cake to write home about. It is ridiculously rich and is the cure-all for those days when your man can't get it right! So call your girlfriends and break out the forks, because it's going to be a long—and delicious—evening!

1 Preheat the oven to 350°F. Grease and flour a 12-cup fluted tube pan, tapping out the excess flour, and set aside.

2 In a large bowl, using an electric mixer on high speed, beat the cake and pudding mixes, oil, and water until well combined. One at a time, beat in the eggs. Add the sour cream, scraping down the sides of the bowl, as needed. Mix until smooth. Using a wooden spoon, stir in the chocolate morsels. Spread evenly in the prepared pan.

3 Bake until the top springs back when pressed lightly in the center, 50 to 55 minutes. Cool cake completely in pan on a wire baking rack.

4 Meanwhile, in a double boiler or in the microwave, melt the chocolate and butter. In a large bowl, combine the confectioners' sugar, vanilla, and ¼ cup of the milk. Blend in the melted chocolate mixture. Add remaining milk, a little at a time, until the frosting reaches the consistency of pancake batter.

5 Spoon the frosting into a resealable plastic bag. Squeeze the air out of the bag and close. Using a pair of scissors, snip one corner of the plastic bag and set aside.

6 Invert the cooled cake onto a cake plate and liberally drizzle with the frosting.

Makes 12 servings

Cake

One 18.25-ounce package devil's food cake

One 3.9-ounce package instant chocolate pudding mix

1 cup vegetable oil

½ cup warm water

4 large eggs

1 cup sour cream

1 cup semisweet chocolate morsels

Frosting

Three 1-ounce squares unsweetened chocolate

8 tablespoons unsalted butter

One 1-pound box confectioners' sugar

½ teaspoon vanilla extract

¾ cup milk

Easy Peach Cobbler

2 cups frozen peaches, thawed

2 cups sugar

¾ cup water

1½ teaspoons cornstarch

1 teaspoon fresh lemon juice

½ teaspoon ground cinnamon

8 tablespoons unsalted butter

¾ cup self-rising flour

¾ cup milk

½ teaspoon vanilla extract

*t*his cobbler is so damn good it comes with a matching drink! If he ever needed confirmation that you are the one, this cobbler is the deal sealer. Top with a scoop of vanilla ice cream or whipped cream, serve him a Peachtini (page 165), and invite us to the wedding!

1 Preheat oven to 350°F.

2 In a medium saucepan over medium-high heat, bring the peaches, 1 cup of the sugar, water, cornstarch, lemon juice, and cinnamon to a boil. Let boil for 1 minute and reduce heat to low. Simmer until the peaches are tender and the sauce starts to thicken, about 10 minutes.

3 In a deep 8 x 8-inch baking dish, melt the butter in the oven.

4 In a medium bowl, mix the remaining 1 cup sugar and the flour. Slowly add milk to the flour mixture and stir just until combined; stir in the vanilla extract.

5 Pour the flour mixture over the melted butter. Do not stir. Spoon the fruit on top and slowly pour in the syrup.

6 Bake until the fruit juices are bubbling and the batter has risen to the top, creating a golden brown crust, 35 to 40 minutes. Serve warm or at room temperature.

Makes 6 servings

Creamy Caramel Cake

*M*oist, buttery caramel cake drizzled with sweet and sticky caramel. Your dentist will hate us—but your man will be sending us testimonials!

1 Preheat the oven to 350°F. Lightly butter and flour three 9-inch cake pans, tapping out the excess flour, and set aside.

2 In a large mixing bowl, using an electric mixer on high, cream together the sugar and butter. Beat until light and fluffy, about 3 minutes. Add the eggs one at a time, mixing well after each addition.

3 In a large bowl, sift together the flour, baking soda, and salt. Reduce mixer speed to low and slowly add the flour mixture to the sugar mixture, alternating with the sour cream. Blend in the vanilla. Pour batter evenly into the prepared pans.

4 Bake until the tops spring back when lightly pressed and a toothpick inserted into the center comes out clean, 25 to 30 minutes. Cool in pans for 10 minutes. Carefully turn the cakes onto a wire cake rack and continue to cool completely.

5 To make the frosting, melt the butter in a medium saucepan over medium heat. Add the brown sugar and milk and bring to a boil, stirring constantly. Let boil for 2 to 3 minutes, then remove from heat.

6 Combine the confectioners' sugar and vanilla in a large mixing bowl, using an electric mixer on low speed. Slowly add the brown sugar mixture and beat until smooth. Let cool slightly. If the frosting is too stiff, add a tablespoon of half-and-half or heavy cream to thin.

7 Spread evenly between layers and on top and sides of cooled cake.

Makes 8 servings

Cake

3 cups granulated sugar

2 sticks (½ pound) unsalted butter, room temperature

6 large eggs, room temperature

2⅔ cups all-purpose flour

¼ teaspoon baking soda

1 teaspoon salt

1 cup sour cream

1 tablespoon vanilla extract

Frosting

1 cup unsalted butter

2 cups light brown sugar, firmly packed

½ cup evaporated milk

One 1-pound box confectioners' sugar

½ teaspoon vanilla extract

Put-It-On-Him Cake

Cake

2 tablespoons light brown sugar

2 teaspoons ground cinnamon

One 18.25-ounce package butter cake mix

½ cup granulated sugar

¾ cup vegetable oil

4 large eggs

1 cup sour cream

½ cup finely chopped pecans

Glaze

1 cup confectioners' sugar

3 tablespoons orange juice

½ teaspoon vanilla extract

*t*he name says it all!

1 Preheat the oven to 350°F. Lightly butter and flour a 9-inch fluted tube pan, tapping out the excess flour, and set aside. Combine the brown sugar and cinnamon in a small bowl and set aside.

2 In a large bowl, using an electric mixer on high speed, beat the cake mix, sugar, and oil until well combined. Beat in the eggs one at a time. Add the sour cream, scraping down the sides of the bowl as needed and mix until smooth. Using a wooden spoon, stir in the pecans.

3 Pour half of the batter into the prepared pan and top with the brown sugar mixture. Spread the remaining batter evenly in the pan.

4 Bake until a toothpick inserted in the cake comes out clean, about 1 hour. Cool in pan for 10 minutes. Carefully turn the cake onto a wire rack and continue to cool completely.

5 In a medium bowl, whisk together the confectioners' sugar, orange juice, and vanilla extract.

6 Drizzle onto the cooled cake.

Makes 8 servings

Like-Sunshine Lemon Cake

*b*righten up his day with this flavorful dessert.

1 Preheat oven to 325°F. Generously butter and flour a 10-inch tube pan, tapping out the excess flour, and set aside.

2 In a large bowl, sift together the flour, baking powder, and salt; set aside.

3 Beat the butter and granulated sugar with an electric mixer on high speed, until mixture is very light and fluffy, about 5 minutes. Beat in the eggs one at a time, scraping down the sides of the bowl as necessary. Blend in the lemon zest.

4 Add flour mixture alternating with the heavy cream. Pour the batter into the prepared cake pan.

5 Bake until a toothpick inserted in the cake comes out clean, about 1 hour. Cool in the pan for 10 minutes. Carefully turn the cake onto a wire rack and continue to cool completely.

6 In a medium bowl, whisk together the glaze ingredients until smooth.

7 Drizzle liberally onto cooled cake.

Makes 10 to 12 servings

Cake

2 cups all-purpose flour

2 teaspoons baking powder

1 teaspoon salt

2 sticks (½ pound) unsalted butter, room temperature

2 cups granulated sugar

3 large eggs

Grated zest of 1 large lemon

1 cup heavy cream

Lemon Glaze

4 tablespoons unsalted butter, melted

2 tablespoons fresh lemon juice

2 cups sifted confectioners' sugar

Crumbly Caramel Apple Pie

Filling and Crust

½ cup packed light brown sugar

2 tablespoons half-and-half

4 tablespoons unsalted butter

½ teaspoon vanilla extract

1 tablespoon plus 1 teaspoon all-purpose flour

Flaky Piecrust (recipe follows)

5 cups peeled Granny Smith apples, cored and thinly sliced

¼ teaspoon lemon juice

⅔ cup granulated sugar

3 tablespoons cornstarch

1 teaspoon ground cinnamon

5 caramel candies, halved

Crumb Topping

⅓ cup granulated sugar

¾ cup all-purpose flour

6 tablespoons unsalted butter, chilled

*a*ll-American? We think not! All Get 'Em Girl! Another signature dessert that comes with Caramel Appletini (page 166) that will have him begging for more.

1 Preheat the oven to 350°F.

2 In a small saucepan over medium heat, cook and stir the brown sugar and half-and-half until the sugar dissolves. Remove from the heat. Add the butter, vanilla, and 1 tablespoon of flour. Stir until the butter melts. Set aside to cool.

3 On a lightly floured work surface, roll out the disk of piecrust dough into a 13-inch round, about ⅛ inch thick. Fold the dough in half. Transfer to a 9-inch pie pan and gently unfold it to fit into the pan. Sprinkle the bottom of the dough with 1 teaspoon of flour.

4 In a large bowl, toss the apples with the lemon juice. Add the granulated sugar, cornstarch, cinnamon, and caramels. Toss to coat the apples. Spoon the apple mixture into the pie pan. Pour the cooled brown sugar sauce over the apples.

5 For the crumb topping, in a medium bowl, mix ⅓ cup sugar with ¾ cup flour. Using a fork, blend the chilled butter into the flour mixture until crumbly. Spoon the crumb topping over the apples, making sure to completely cover them. Using a knife or scissors, trim the edges of the bottom piecrust so it hangs over just about 1 inch. Fold the dough under itself so the edge of the fold is flush with the edge of the pie pan. Crimp the crust around the edges of the pan with a fork.

6 Cover the pie with aluminum foil and place on a baking sheet. Bake for 25 minutes. Remove the foil and bake until golden brown and the juices are bubbling, 20 to 25 minutes. Cool completely on a wire rack.

Makes 8 servings

Flaky Piecrust

In a medium bowl, sift the flour and salt together. Using a fork, blend the shortening into the flour until the mixture resembles small peas. Stirring with the fork, gradually add just enough of the water to make the mixture clump together. Gather up the dough and press into a thick disk.

1½ cups all-purpose flour

½ teaspoon salt

½ cup vegetable shortening, chilled

⅓ cup ice water

TAKE NOTE

For extra tender piecrust, do not overwork the dough. Chilling the shortening and water will help to make this piecrust flaky.

Just Peachy Bread Pudding

Bread Pudding

2½ cups diced peeled peaches (fresh or frozen)

¼ cup peach nectar

4 slices brioche bread, crusts removed, cut into 1-inch cubes (4 cups)

3 tablespoons unsalted butter, melted

½ cup golden raisins

3 large eggs

½ cup granulated sugar

1 teaspoon ground cinnamon

1¾ cups half-and-half

1 teaspoon vanilla extract

Brown Sugar–Vanilla Sauce

½ cup light brown sugar

2 tablespoons light corn syrup (recommended: Karo)

4 tablespoons unsalted butter

½ cup heavy cream

1½ teaspoons vanilla extract

1 Preheat the oven to 325°F. Lightly butter a 2½-quart baking dish and set aside.

2 In a medium saucepan over medium-low heat, bring the peaches and peach nectar to a simmer. Cook until peaches are tender, about 5 minutes.

3 In a large bowl, gently toss the bread, melted butter, raisins, and peaches until the bread is completely coated. In a separate large bowl, whisk together the eggs, granulated sugar, cinnamon, half-and-half, and 1 teaspoon vanilla extract. Add the bread mixture and mix gently. Pour into prepared dish.

4 Bake until golden brown and the center is set, about 1 hour.

5 In a small saucepan, over medium heat, combine the brown sugar, corn syrup, butter, cream, and vanilla extract. Bring to a boil, stirring frequently. Reduce the heat to medium-low and cook for 5 minutes, stirring continually. Remove from the heat. The sauce will thicken as it cools. Drizzle over the top of bread pudding and serve warm or at room temperature.

Makes 4 to 6 servings

Peachtini

Pour all ingredients in a cocktail shaker half filled with ice cubes. Shake vigorously and strain into martini glasses.

Makes 2 servings

½ cup coconut rum

½ cup peach-flavored vodka

½ cup ginger ale

Caramel Appletini

½ cup vodka

½ cup apple schnapps

½ cup butterscotch schnapps

Pour all ingredients in a cocktail shaker half filled with ice cubes. Shake vigorously and strain into martini glasses.

Makes 2 servings

In Love 'n' Health

My Suga's Got Sugar! Menu

Grilled Garlic Steak

Smothered Chops

Perfectly Baked Brown Rice

Candied Carrots

Mixed Berry Parfait

What Do You Mean, No More Meat? Menu

Tempeh Chili

Kirsten's Vegetable Lasagna

Sesame-Soy Pasta and Vegetables

Tawanda's Vegan Carrot Cake with Faux Cream Cheese Frosting

Baby, I Don't Care What the Doctor Says, Your Keg Is Sexy! Menu

Oven-Fried Flounder

Sweet Potato Fries

"Spaghetti" with Meat Sauce

Yes-They're-Good-for-You Oatmeal Cookies

*n*ow that you have found the man of your dreams and you have resolved that he is the Ossie to your Ruby, you want him around as long as possible. Whether you're pushing him out the door for personal training sessions, or working out together in the park, the key to good health is a balance of exercise and proper diet. Since the two of you are madly in love, we are pretty sure you're getting in more than enough exercise (wink), so let us take care of the food. We don't think you should forfeit taste to make the dishes healthful, so we came up with some delicious and healthful meals that you and your partner will love!

For the most part, the dishes highlighted in this chapter fall under one of three categories: low-fat, low-carb/sugar, or meat-free; so feel free to pick and choose from each section to come up with a meal your sweetie won't believe could actually be good for him.

Grilled Garlic Steak

*i*t is all about the marinade with this steak. The longer you let it marinate, the better it will taste.

1 In a small bowl, mix the olive oil, soy sauce, vinegar, ketchup, and garlic. Place flank steak in a large resealable plastic bag. Pour marinade over steak. Seal and refrigerate for at least 3 hours.

2 Heat a grill pan over medium-high heat. Place steak on the grill and discard marinade. Cook for 5 minutes on each side for medium-rare. Remove from heat to a cutting board and let rest for 3 minutes, allowing juices to redistribute.

3 Slice the steak into ¼-inch-thick strips, against the grain of the meat, before serving.

Makes 4 servings

¼ cup extra virgin olive oil

¼ cup low-sodium soy sauce

4½ teaspoons distilled white vinegar

2 tablespoons ketchup

2 tablespoons chopped garlic

1½ pounds flank or sirloin steak

Smothered Chops

4 turkey cutlets or boneless pork chops, ½ inch thick

½ teaspoon salt

½ teaspoon ground black pepper

¼ cup self-rising flour

⅓ cup canola oil

1 medium onion, chopped

2 cloves garlic, chopped

½ cup chopped green bell pepper

½ cup chopped tomato

½ teaspoon peeled and grated fresh ginger

1 teaspoon fresh thyme leaves

2 tablespoons low-sodium soy sauce

1 chicken bouillon cube, dissolved in ⅓ cup water

a diabetic-friendly variation to our suffocated pork chops—and they are just as good.

1 Season the chops with salt and pepper, then lightly coat with flour and set aside.

2 Heat the canola oil in a large skillet over medium heat. Carefully add the chops to the skillet and fry 6 to 7 minutes on each side, until lightly browned.

3 Stir in the onion, garlic, bell pepper, tomato, ginger, thyme, soy sauce, and bouillon mixture. Reduce the heat to low and cover. Simmer until chops are cooked through and tender, 25 to 30 minutes. Remove from heat and serve hot with Perfectly Baked Brown Rice (following page).

Makes 2 to 4 servings

Perfectly Baked Brown Rice

Preheat the oven to 375°F. Place the rice in an 8 x 8-inch baking dish. In a medium saucepan, bring the water, butter (if using), salt, and pepper to a boil. Once the water begins to boil, remove from heat and pour over the rice. Stir to combine and cover the dish tightly with aluminum foil. Bake on the middle rack for 1 hour. Remove from oven and fluff rice with a fork. Serve hot.

Makes 4 to 6 servings

1 cup brown rice

2 cups water

1 tablespoon unsalted butter (optional)

1 teaspoon salt

¼ teaspoon ground black pepper

Candied Carrots

1 pound baby carrots

2 tablespoons unsalted butter, melted

2 tablespoons Splenda Brown Sugar Blend

Salt and ground black pepper

1 Place the carrots in a pot of lightly salted water and bring to a boil over medium-high heat. Reduce the heat to medium-low and simmer for 15 to 20 minutes, making sure not to overcook.

2 Drain the carrots, reduce heat to low, and return carrots to the pot. Stir in the butter, Splenda, and salt and pepper to taste. Cook until the sugar is bubbly, 3 to 5 minutes. Remove from heat and let stand for 2 minutes. Serve hot.

Makes 2 to 4 servings

Mixed Berry Parfait

*t*his is a quick and easy way to complete any meal with the light taste of sweet berries. You can use fresh seasonal berries or frozen ones, whatever works for you.

1 In a small bowl, mix the yogurt and Splenda until well combined. Cover the bottoms of two small glasses with a layer of yogurt. Cover the yogurt with 1½ teaspoons of granola and top with the berries.

2 Repeat layers, until both glasses are full. Sprinkle top with granola and serve immediately.

Makes 2 servings

Two 8-ounce containers plain yogurt

2 teaspoons Splenda Granular Sweetener

2 tablespoons plus 1½ teaspoons low-fat granola

One 10-ounce package frozen mixed berries, thawed

Tempeh Chili

2 tablespoons vegetable oil

One 8-ounce package tempeh, crumbled

1 large onion, diced

One 8-ounce can red kidney beans, rinsed and drained

One 8-ounce can whole peeled tomatoes, hand-crushed

1½ cups tomato sauce

¼ cup chili powder

1 teaspoon cumin

1 teaspoon garlic powder

2 cups hot cooked rice

Heat the vegetable oil in a large saucepan over medium heat. Add the tempeh. Cook and stir until lightly browned, about 10 minutes. Reduce the heat to low and add the onion, beans, tomatoes, tomato sauce, chili powder, cumin, and garlic powder. Simmer for 20 minutes. Remove from heat. Serve immediately over rice.

Makes 6 servings

TAKE NOTE

Tempeh is a fermented food made from soybeans. Unlike tofu, tempeh is made from the whole soybean and contains a high protein, dietary fiber, and vitamin content. It has the texture, appearance, and consistency of meat, which makes it great for a vegetarian Bolognese sauce, stews, and other "meat"-based vegetarian dishes.

Kirsten's Vegetable Lasagna

*f*resh vegetables, layered with mozzarella and ricotta cheese.

1 Preheat the oven to 375°F. Spray a 13 x 9 x 3-inch deep baking pan with nonstick cooking spray.

2 In a medium bowl, beat the eggs. Stir in the ricotta, 2 cups of the mozzarella, and the Parmesan. Season with salt and pepper.

3 Pour the olive oil into a large skillet over medium-high heat. Add the onions and garlic; cook and stir until the onions are translucent, about 5 minutes.

4 Place the spinach in a colander and squeeze until all the liquid is out of spinach. Add the spinach to the skillet and toss to coat. Cook and stir for 2 minutes and remove from heat. Season to taste with salt and pepper.

5 To assemble: start with a thin layer of sauce on the bottom of the lasagna pan, about ½ cup. Layer with 4 uncooked lasagna noodles (slightly overlapping if necessary). Next, add one-third of ricotta cheese mixture, one-third of the sautéed spinach mixture, and 1 cup of sauce. Repeat with two more layers of noodles, ricotta cheese mixture, spinach, and sauce. Finish with a layer of noodles spread with sauce, and top with remaining mozzarella cheese. Cover with aluminum foil.

6 Bake until the sauce begins to bubble around the edges of the lasagna and the noodles are tender, about 45 minutes. Remove from oven and let rest for 10 minutes. Serve with a Quick Side Salad (page 108).

Makes 6 to 8 servings

2 large eggs

One 15-ounce container ricotta cheese

4 cups shredded mozzarella cheese

½ cup freshly grated Parmesan cheese

Salt and ground black pepper

3 tablespoons olive oil

1 small onion, finely diced

2 cloves garlic, minced

1 pound frozen spinach, thawed

One 9-ounce box uncooked lasagna noodles (recommended: Barilla No-Boil Lasagne

4 cups Easy Tomato Sauce (page 115)

Sesame-Soy Pasta and Vegetables

1½ cups vegetable broth

8 ounces medium no-yolk noodles

2 cups small fresh broccoli florets

1 cup sliced button mushrooms

2 medium carrots, peeled and sliced thin on the diagonal

2 tablespoons low-sodium soy sauce

1 tablespoon cornstarch

1 tablespoon sesame oil

2 teaspoons sugar

¼ teaspoon red pepper flakes

*t*his quick and easy meal is sure to satisfy all of your dinner guests. Your vegetarian dates will appreciate it!

Bring the vegetable broth to a boil in a large pot over high heat. Add the noodles to the pot; cover and reduce heat to a low. Cook until noodles are just tender, about 8 minutes. Add the vegetables and continue to cook for 2 minutes. In a small bowl, combine the soy sauce, cornstarch, sesame oil, sugar, and red pepper flakes; slowly stir into pot. Stir until well combined and thickened. Serve immediately.

Makes 4 servings

Tawanda's Vegan Carrot Cake with Faux Cream Cheese Frosting

1 In a medium bowl, mix the brown sugar and shredded carrots. Cover with plastic wrap and set aside for 1 hour.

2 Preheat the oven to 350°F. Grease and flour two 10-inch cake pans and set aside.

3 In a medium bowl, sift together the flour, baking soda, salt, cinnamon, and allspice and set aside.

4 In a large bowl, using an electric mixer on high speed, beat the egg replacement until light. Gradually beat in the cane sugar, vegetable and coconut oils, and the vanilla extract until well combined.

5 Reduce mixer speed to low and beat in the flour mixture, scraping down the sides of the bowl as needed. Mix just until smooth. Using a wooden spoon, stir in the shredded carrot mixture. Spread batter evenly in the prepared pans.

6 Bake until the top springs back when pressed lightly in the center, 45 to 50 minutes. Cool for 10 minutes and remove from pans. Cool completely on a wire rack.

7 In a medium bowl, using an electric mixer, beat the vegan cream cheese and margarine until smooth. Add the vanilla extract and confectioners' sugar and continue to beat until smooth. Place one cake layer on desired cake dish, then frost cake. Add second layer on top and frost. Spread the frosting over the top and sides of the cake.

Makes 10 to 12 servings

Cake

1 cup vegan light brown cane sugar

6 cups shredded carrots

3 cups all-purpose flour

2 teaspoons baking soda

1 teaspoon salt

1 teaspoon ground cinnamon

2 teaspoons ground allspice

3-egg equivalent of vegan egg replacer (recommended: Ener-G)

1 cup vegan cane sugar

½ cup vegetable oil

½ cup coconut oil

2 teaspoons vanilla extract

Frosting

One 8-ounce package vegan cream cheese, room temperature

⅓ cup vegan soy margarine, room temperature (recommended: Earth Balance)

1 teaspoon vanilla extract

2 cups vegan confectioners' sugar

Oven-Fried Flounder

½ cup fat-free milk

½ teaspoon salt

½ cup yellow cornmeal

3 tablespoons plain dry bread crumbs

½ teaspoon Get 'Em Girls' Essential Seasoning (page 29)

⅛ teaspoon ground black pepper

¼ teaspoon sweet paprika

⅛ teaspoon cayenne pepper

4 flounder fillets, about 4 ounces each

1 tablespoon unsalted butter, melted

*g*ive your frying pan a break and try this light and crispy dish. Make it a heart-healthy fish and chips meal with Sweet Potato Fries (following page)

1 Preheat the oven to 500°F. Spray a baking dish with nonstick cooking spray.

2 In a shallow dish, mix the milk and salt and set aside. In a separate bowl, combine the cornmeal, bread crumbs, Seasoning, black pepper, paprika, and cayenne pepper. Dip the fish fillets in the milk and then roll in the cornmeal mixture.

3 Place the fish in the prepared baking dish. Pour the melted butter over the fish and bake 10 to 15 minutes until the fish flakes easily when tested with a fork.

Makes 4 servings

Sweet Potato Fries

1 Preheat the oven to 450°F. Spray a cookie sheet with nonstick cooking spray.

2 Cut the sweet potatoes lengthwise into quarters, then cut each quarter lengthwise into two wedges. Arrange the potatoes in a single layer on the cookie sheet.

3 In a small saucepan over medium heat, melt the butter. Add the Seasoning, pepper, and nutmeg. Brush this mixture onto potatoes. Bake for 20 minutes or until brown and tender.

Makes 4 servings

4 small unpeeled sweet potatoes, washed and scrubbed

1 tablespoon unsalted butter

¼ teaspoon Get 'Em Girls' Essential Seasoning (page 29)

⅛ teaspoon ground black pepper

Dash of freshly ground nutmeg

"Spaghetti" with Meat Sauce

2 tablespoons extra virgin olive oil, plus more for drizzling

1 pound ground turkey

¼ cup chopped onion

¼ cup chopped green bell pepper

1 clove garlic, chopped

½ cup sliced crimini mushrooms

Two 15-ounce cans stewed tomatoes

1 tablespoon tomato paste

1 tablespoon dried thyme

1 tablespoon Italian seasoning blend

1 tablespoon dried oregano

Dash of red pepper flakes

2 teaspoons Splenda Granular Sweetener (optional)

1 medium spaghetti squash

Salt and ground black pepper

*S*ubstitute pasta with spaghetti squash for a low-carb comfort food that will have him fueled and fit in no time.

1 Heat the olive oil in a large saucepan over medium heat. Add the ground turkey, onions, green peppers, garlic, and mushrooms. Cook, stirring frequently, until brown. Do not drain.

2 Stir in the tomatoes, tomato paste, thyme, Italian seasoning blend, and oregano. Bring to a boil. Add the red pepper flakes and Splenda (if using). Reduce heat to low and simmer for 1 hour.

3 Meanwhile, bring a large stockpot of lightly salted water to a boil. Slice the squash in half lengthwise. Scoop out the seeds with a spoon. Completely submerge both halves in boiling water and cook until the inside is fork tender and pulls apart into strands, 15 to 20 minutes.

4 Remove the squash from the pot; drain and cool with cold water. Using a fork, scrape the cooked squash out of its skin, fluffing and separating into spaghetti-like strands. Discard the skin. Drizzle with olive oil and season with salt and pepper.

5 Spoon the meat sauce over the spaghetti squash and serve immediately.

Makes 4 servings

Yes-They're-Good-for-You Oatmeal Cookies

a delicious and healthful version of the traditional oatmeal cookie. With the addition of applesauce, this is an extremely moist and almost cakelike cookie.

1 Preheat oven to 350°F. Butter a cookie sheet and set aside.

2 Beat the butter and Splenda Brown Sugar Blend in a large bowl with an electric mixer until creamy. Add the eggs and mix well. With a large spoon, mix in the applesauce until well combined.

3 In a separate bowl, sift together the flour, salt, cinnamon, and baking soda. Add the oats and the flour mixture into the applesauce mixture and mix well. Fold in the raisins and the vanilla extract.

4 In batches, drop by rounded teaspoons onto the prepared cookie sheet. Bake for 10 to 12 minutes. Remove from oven and let cool completely on a wire cake rack before serving.

Makes about 2 dozen cookies

4 tablespoons unsalted butter

1 cup Splenda Brown Sugar Blend

2 large eggs

½ cup unsweetened applesauce

2 cups whole-wheat flour

1 teaspoon salt

1 teaspoon ground cinnamon

1 teaspoon baking soda

2 cups quick-cooking oats

1 cup raisins

2 teaspoons vanilla extract

You Got Him ... Now What?

*i*f this were a perfect world, all the ills of a relationship would be solved with the whiff of freshly baked peach cobbler. Unfortunately, this is not a perfect world and relationships require more than a banging cobbler recipe. In fact, relationships take quite a bit of work, but anything worth having is worth working for.

So, while you are putting in work in the kitchen, don't forget to keep the relationship fun, fresh, and sexy. Just in case you need a little help (which we are sure you don't) here are a few tips to guide you:

Issue: Against your parents' advice, the two of you decided to get an apartment together. The once sex-filled nights (and mornings) have suddenly turned into reality . . . and it bites! You realize quickly that love is so much sexier when you are not picking up his dirty socks from the living room floor.

Answer: Spice things up! Toss your good-girl image to the wind and let him know you are not to be played with! Turn your love nest into an erotic red-light district, complete with a removable dance pole (we would give you the Web address . . . but we can't be held responsible if you break your neck!) and fare easily devoured off of or drizzled deliciously on you. If nothing else, we bet he will be picking up behind himself in no time.

Issue: You just got the promotion of your dreams; the corner office is to die for, the stock options are orgasmic, and the salary is . . . well let's just say, your Hot Plate Love days are over. Unfortunately, like the saying goes "with great power, comes great responsibility" . . . and your relationship is suffering. Your man hasn't seen you in a week and he is wondering if you forgot about him . . . even your Shih Tzu thought you were an intruder and went Cujo on your butt; what do you do?

Answer: Play hooky! Wake up early and start by treating your love (and your dog) to breakfast in bed—don't forget the mimosas, you're not going to work today! Turn off your BlackBerry—wait, just put it on vibrate . . . and treat him to a day planned just for him. Whether it's a picnic for two or a trip to his favorite bookstore . . . make sure it's something that he likes and is interested in. Enjoy him for the entire day, without interruption, and let him know that your career is not the only priority in your life.

Issue: You are tired! Food is what you need, but cooking is the last thing on your mind. Guess who just called asking "What's for dinner, baby?"
Answer: Take a deep breath—now let your fingers get to dialing! Hey, even Get 'Em Girls do take-out every now and then. Let him know you will order the pizza and fix the salad while he can pick the wine and movie. Keep it simple, don't sweat it, and even if you didn't make it . . . you can still work it.

Issue: The two of you have been on a relationship whirlwind for the past three months, nothing else matters in the world except the two of you . . . and then, he asks you to meet his friends. You've heard all the stories about Mark's college days as a stripper and Derrick's insane ex-girlfriend crashing every event he attends—in fact, I'm sure you even confided in him some stories about your girlfriends that you are praying to God he doesn't mention in their presence. How do you handle it?
Answer: Make it a party! The late, great Notorious B.I.G. said it best: "Tell your friends, to get with my friends—we can al7l be friends . . ." and you know if there's any time to show off your new culinary skills—now is that time! Keep it simple and invite your closest friends, the ones whose opinions matter the most to you and you know won't act a straight fool when they meet your sweetie. Just be yourself, keep the menu simple, and the pillow-talk you both shared to yourselves and we are sure everything will turn out fine.

Index